Feasting in the Forest

by
Dave and Nancy Brannon

Illustrated by Patti Boyd
Published by Dave and Nancy Brannon

First Edition 1989

ISBN 0-9623036-0-7

Library of Congress Catalogue Number 89-91608

Written, designed and published by
Dave and Nancy Brannon, Cody, Wyoming

Type set in "Belwe" by Dwight Yaeger, Typographer, Inc.

Lithography by Thompson-Shore, Inc.

DEDICATION

To our friends, Sandra and Ragnar Hartman, whose support, encouragement, and help, enabled us to make it thru the blood, sweat, and tears of the early years—with laughter and love.

To Christene Cosgriffe Meyers, Arts and Travel Editor of the Billings Gazette, whose discovery of us and subsequent wonderful feature article in her "ENJOY" magazine put us on the map.

. . . And . . .

To our incredible Patrons, who come from 46 states and 17 foreign countries, thru rain, sleet, snow and mud, to make our efforts worthwhile. You are gracious, kind, sophisticated, and loyal—our greatest inspiration!

ACKNOWLEDGEMENT

Many, many thanks to our friend and mentor, Franca Facchetti.
She has patiently tried to teach us the Italian language. The net result, is that we speak "food". We've always said that when in Italy, we'd have trouble asking directions or hailing a taxi...but we'd have NO trouble ordering in a restaurant!

Not only has she worked with us over the last couple of years on our pronunciation and grammar, but she personally proof-read all of the Italian words in this book. Accuracy and authenticity are very important to us . . . we could not have done so well without her help.

TABLE OF CONTENTS

THE WINDING DIRT MOUNTAIN ROAD

Years ago, in Texas, a friend took me to his favorite steakhouse in the hill country north of San Antonio. We drove out of town, turned off the highway onto a farm road, then turned onto a gravel road that wound thru the woods to a little old shack with smoke curling up from the cookstove chimney.

I often recall the magic of that evening when we turn off the highway to come home.

Our lodge happens to be the most remote facility of its kind in any forest in the lower 48 states. Three and a half miles of winding dirt mountain road can be a real challenge to folks who've only driven on pavement.

We put up two signs along the way so our patrons would not get discouraged. Simple little signs, but important.

Time after time folks tell us when they came to the first sign, which reads "Brannon's 2 miles", they were

convinced they'd already driven five. Then they drive what seems another three miles and come to the next sign, which reads "Brannon's 1 mile". Thereafter, they seem to grit their teeth, grab the steering wheel with renewed determination, and penetrate deeper into the wilderness in search of our gateway.

It really is a wonderful road—a wilderness road.

These are the Rocky Mountains and they didn't get that name as a whim of some early explorer. These mountains are rugged, spectacular and very different from those back east.

The youngest mountain chain on earth, barely ten million years old, the Rockies are still rising at the rate of nearly 3 inches per year. The erosion forces of wind and weather have not had the opportunity to round and soften these peaks to the degree apparent in the eastern chains . . . hundreds of millions of years older.

Soon after entering the Shoshone National Forest, on the road to Yellowstone National Park, turn north thru the Wapiti Campground. Drive thru the campground to the northfork of the Shoshone River and you will come to an arch bridge spanning the river. Cross the bridge and you will discover the road is, from that point on, dirt and single lane.

You'll pass thru King Sage, so-called because it grows to six feet or more, then climb slowly as the road twists and turns over the east face of the cliffs guarding the mouth of beautiful Sweetwater Canyon.

The road descends to the canyon floor, then follows Sweetwater Creek thru a stand of 200 year old Douglas fir, before starting the long winding climb to the end of the road at, "Brannon's".

Before you reach the closed gate at the corrals, thru which only those with confirmed reservations may pass, you will cross the creek twice on narrow wooden bridges. The road crosses to the west side of the canyon then back to the east side near the one mile marker.

Throughout your journey, if you trust the driver's skill enough to take your eyes off the road, you will be treated to an abundance of big game sightings. You are, after all, a guest in the home of deer, elk, moose, big horn sheep, black and grizzly bear, and, the elusive cougar (or mountain lion).

Thanks to our wonderful and adventurous road, just getting to Brannon's, is half the fun!

TO BEGIN WITH . . .

As the title suggests, this is both a cookbook and a chronicle. It is a compilation of many of the dishes we have served our guests, coupled with anecdotes of true adventures we experienced in this spectacular wilderness.

The chapters follow much the same order as the courses in our feast...only slightly different from that served in Italy. For instance, the Italians more often serve pasta as a first course...only occasionally with the meat course. We have combined them in our feasts, so that we could offer as much variety as possible in eight courses.

All recipes, with the few exceptions noted, are authentic and original. Authentic ...in tradition and origin, and original...in that we have tailored them to reflect our patron's wishes.

We bought this old abandoned lodge during our courtship. We envisioned its restoration and ultimate purpose before we signed the buy/sell agreement. We finalized our plan of action on our honeymoon. From its conception, to this very moment, it epitomizes our "labor of love".

To you, the reader, we make this pledge...every recipe has been faithfully reproduced to the highest degree of exactitude within our power, so that you may, by following each recipe to the letter, be assured of its authenticity. And, if you are a patron who has already tasted the dish, you can re-live that first experience.

Buon Appetito!

SPEAKING OF INGREDIENTS

OLIVE OIL: With rare exception, our recipes call for "extra virgin" olive oil. Extra virgin olive oils provide a wide range of flavors, from light and delicate, to fruity and flavorful, and the prices, like fine wines, vary also. You are more assured of a fine quality olive oil if you choose "extra virgin" than if you select a lesser grade.

All olive oils are cholesterol free, and are good for you when used sparingly. We use them for nearly everything (except deep frying) even baking.

Ninety percent of Italy's olive oil is produced in Sicily. You might want to experiment with several brands...one for salads...one for baking...and so on!

GARLIC: Whenever possible, use fresh garlic. Most of our recipes containing garlic, call for a specific measurement of "minced" garlic, so that you don't have to guess about the size of a "clove" of garlic, which varies widely. You can find minced fresh garlic by the jar in the produce department of most supermarkets. In addition to being incredibly convenient, it keeps well in the refrigerator for several weeks.

HERBS: Fresh herbs are, far and away, superior to dried herbs. We grow most of our herbs fresh here at the lodge. Not only do they taste better, but growing them is great fun...and very little effort considering the rewards. A small window box will do...or a corner of your seasonal garden.

Remember to DOUBLE the quantity shown for dried herbs, if you are using fresh ones. As herbs are dried, they shrink in size, but not in their intensity. Therefore, it takes only half as much dried herb, to equal one portion of fresh herb.

In some recipes, like our PESTO ALLA GENOVESE, fresh herbs are essential. Substituting dried herbs just doesn't work!

BUTTER and CREAM: We always use sweet creamery butter, (lightly salted), and heavy whipping cream. The flavors cannot be duplicated with margarine and low fat milk. We encourage you, however, to go ahead with margarine and low fat milk if you have special health or dietary needs. While the flavors are not the same, you can still turn out a flavorful and pleasing dish in most cases. But, if you really want to duplicate the dish exactly as it was served on the feast...real cream and butter are "musts".

VEGETABLES: As with herbs, the key here is "fresh". If the vegetable you wish to use is out-of-season, then use frozen...far superior to canned, with one exception. A good quality whole, peeled, canned tomato, beats a pale, tasteless, pink "winter" tomato any day! And, there are certain products, like canned artichoke hearts, that are preferable because they are so convenient.

MUSHROOMS: NEVER use canned mushrooms! Always use fresh ones! And, if you are fortunate enough to be able to buy them...fresh porcini, morel, or shitake mushrooms are fabulous.

PARMESAN CHEESE: The deli department of your supermarket most likely carries a variety of Parmesan cheeses...by the piece. NEVER buy Parmesan that's already been grated. Grate your own fresh. If you can find it...Parmigiano Reggiano...the "Rolls Royce" of Parmesans...or Grana Padano...the "Cadillac" ...should be the brand you choose. The flavor of either one is so wonderful, you'll want to serve them, as the Italians do, in slivers along with fresh fruit.

PROSCIUTTO: Prosciutto, or Parma Ham, has a very unique flavor and texture. It comes from northern Italy, and its production is carefully controlled by the Italian government, to assure consistent excellent quality. Boiled ham may be substituted in some cases, but the flavor cannot compare. A better substitution is Smithfield Ham, if you can find one. Whatever you use, have your butcher slice it wafer thin for best results.

Appetizers

OPENING NIGHT GRIZZLY BEAR

Look at a map of Yellowstone National Park and you will see the park is surrounded by National Forests. The park and forests comprise "The Yellowstone Ecosystem".

Our lodge is located in the very heart of Shoshone National Forest. It used to be part of the Yellowstone Timber Preserve, but in 1905 it was designated our nation's first National Forest.

Of all the forests surrounding the park, only the Shoshone boasts co-ownership with Yellowstone of the majestic Absaroka Mountains . . . that massive range of the Rocky Mountains that kept the mysterious, awesome, and beautiful wonders of Yellowstone a secret from the white man for nearly four centuries after Columbus discovered America . . . the finest Grizzly bear habitat in the lower 48 states!

For many years the Grizzly bear has been on the Endangered Species List and the subject of intense research and preservation efforts of both the federal and state authorities. A few years ago they joined forces in a cooperative effort . . . the Interagency Grizzly Bear Study Team . . . and have achieved a high degree of success. (I can testify to that! My son, Robert was on the team!)

It was near the end of May, after many months of toil, before we were able to restore and open the lodge for our first feast. We had bought the lodge the previous December when, if there were any bears in our part of the forest, they would be asleep.   If bears had been on our mind opening night, which they weren't, our thoughts would have been of the Black bear . . . certainly not the endangered Grizzly.

In a misguided effort to be efficient, I had earlier in the day emptied the bear-proof trash container into the pickup for the next day's run to the dump, some 38 miles away. The pickup was parked in its usual place . . . the patron's parking lot behind the lodge.

During the evening a warm rain began, and after the feast, our guests lingered by the fireplace prolonging goodbyes. I was by an open window in the corner of the dining room when suddenly I heard our big black Labrador named "Rodie", confined to his kennel when guests were present, barking quite insistently . . . which more annoyed than alerted me. I decided to accompany our guests to their cars so I could call to him to quiet his barking.

The moment we stepped outside onto the lodge porch I knew Rodie's barking was signaling something new to him and something he considered a threat. So I asked our guests to step back into the lodge while I investigated.

I grabbed a flashlight and started around the lodge. The batteries were very weak and the beam only reached ahead a few feet. As I rounded the corner, I heard a great deal of clamor in the back of the pickup . . . banging of cans, tearing of boxes and bags...but my light would not reach that far. I shone the light about my feet until I could find a good sized rock to heave at the pickup. A bear, I was now certain, was our problem.

I heard the rock hit the truck body with a loud bang and the commotion in the back stopped. At the same time our guests, who had ventured back onto the lodge porch, began yelling after me as to what I had found. Between the dog-barking, the rock-throwing, and the human sounds . . . certainly not the weak beam of the flashlight . . . the bear decided he'd had enough to eat and may as well head on up the canyon.

In the morning's light we learned with certainty that, not only was our uninvited guest a bear, it was a Grizzly. Over the top of the cab and straight down the center of the hood, were perfect textbook tracks of "Ursus Arctos Horribilus" himself! The warm rain had muddied the parking area and, at the same time, cleaned the surface of the truck, readying it for his unique signature.

When next we went to town, we parked the truck in front of Cody's only hotel, so all could enjoy our prize.

Thereafter, I loaded the pickup, for the run to the dump, with the motor running and my shopping list on the seat, so as not to delay our departure for a moment!

9

CARCIOFI E FORMAGGIO AL FORNO
Baked Artichoke Spread with Cheese

A quick and easy appetizer you bake and serve bubbling hot!

1 cup of real Mayonnaise (not salad dressing)
(or try our recipe for MAIONESE DI LIMONE)
1 cup of grated Parmesan Cheese
1 14-ounce can of Artichoke Hearts (plain, not marinated)
(drained and coarsely chopped)

Simply combine the three ingredients and place them in an oven-proof baking dish. Put them in a preheated 375 degree oven for approximately 30 minutes, or until golden brown and bubbly on top.

SERVING SUGGESTION: About 10 minutes before the spread is due to come out of the oven, slide a loaf of brown and serve French bread in the oven along side the spread. When both are done, place the hot baking dish into a napkin-lined basket, and surround it with slices of the warm French bread. Serve hot.

SPECIAL TIP: You can make this mixture up to a full day ahead, so you can spend time with your guests when they arrive. Just take it out of the refrigerator...and pop it in the oven!

STORAGE INFORMATION: Mixture can be stored UNBAKED in the refrigerator for up to a day ahead.

PREPARATION TIME: 40 minutes

YIELD: About 2 cups of spread

POLENTA ALLA LODIGIANA
Polenta Appetizers in the style of Lodi

A delicious addition to an antipasto tray, this hot and tasty treat is quite nourishing, too!

1 recipe of POLENTA
4 ounces of Asiago Cheese (Mozzarella works well, too!)
1 Whole Egg, lightly beaten
Enough Bread Crumbs for coating (1 cup, or more)
Vegetable Oil for deep frying

Make the POLENTA, and while it's still hot, spread it in a jelly roll pan lined with plastic wrap. Set aside to cool. Using a small cookie cutter (1 ¼ to 1 ½ inches in diameter)…cut rounds of the POLENTA and of the cheese and make "sandwiches". (If you don't have a cookie cutter that small…a cordial glass works very well!) Holding them together, dip the "sandwiches" into the beaten egg and then roll them in the bread crumbs. Set aside. Heat enough oil in a deep skillet to approximately 375 degrees. Fry the POLENTA ALLA LODIGIANA four or five at a time holding them in a warm oven until all of them are fried and ready to serve. Serve hot.

NOTE: If you're nervous about the sandwiches staying together during the cooking process, simply skewer them with a wooden toothpick before deep frying. The heat won't harm the toothpick, and they make a convenient "handle" for eating!

SPECIAL TIP: The rounds of POLENTA are fairly easy to get out of the cordial glass, simply by tapping the side of the glass on the palm of your hand. The cheese is a little trickier, however! To make this easy and fast, just have the cheese at room temperature when you cut it. Then lift the circle out with the tip of a sharp knife.

STORAGE INFORMATION: The POLENTA can be made several days ahead and stored in the refrigerator. Then, the day of your gathering, make up the POLENTA ALLA LODIGIANA…place them on a tray lined with wax paper. Cover them with plastic wrap and store, refrigerated, until ready to deep fry.

PREPARATION TIME: 30 to 40 minutes (excluding preparation of POLENTA itself)

YIELD: 24 pieces

FONDI DI CARCIOFI CON MAIONESE E ROSA DI POMODORO
Artichoke Bottom with Tarragon Mayonnaise and Tomato Rose

While an extremely simple recipe, the combination of flavors is elegant, and the presenatation lovely!

2 - 13¾ ounce cans of Artichoke Bottoms (not "hearts")

(each can will contain 5 to 7 bottoms)

1 cup of real Mayonnaise

(or, make your own with my recipe for MAIONAISE AL LIMONE)

1½ teaspoons Tarragon

½ teaspoon Lemon Juice

5 large ripe Tomatoes

Drain and rinse the artichoke bottoms...pat dry with paper towels. Combine mayonnaise, tarragon and lemon juice, blending well. Put 1 rounded teaspoon of Tarragon Mayonnaise into each artichoke bottom...set aside. FOR TOMATO ROSES: With a very sharp knife, "peel" the tomato, taking some of the flesh, too (but not too thick!)...making one complete revolution for each rose needed. (You should get 3 roses from each tomato.) Roll the strips up, turning the skin side IN...twisting them into a a fairly tight spiral. And there you have it! A tomato rose! Nestle the Tomato Roses in the top of the filled artichoke bottoms and serve chilled.

SPECIAL TIP: The left-over peeled tomatoes are very nice for salads, of course. But, if you have no immediate need for them, cut the stem end out with a paring knife...put the tomatoes into a plastic freezer bag and freeze them for later! The texture after freezing will not be suitable for salads, but they still work very well in soups and sauces!

STORAGE INFORMATION: May be made up several hours ahead of time...just cover with plastic wrap and refrigerate.

PREPARATION TIME: 15 minutes

YIELD: 10 to 14 pieces

FUNGHI MARINATI
Marinated Mushrooms

A delightful addition to any antipasto tray! This same basic recipe and method can be applied to a variety of vegetables...like artichoke hearts!

1 pound Fresh Mushrooms
½ cup Extra Virgin Olive Oil
2 tablespoons Lemon Juice
Garlic Salt to taste
1 teaspoon dried Basil (or 2 teaspoons of FRESH)
2 tablespoons Sweet Red or Yellow Pepper, coarsely chopped
Freshly ground Black Pepper to taste

Never wash mushrooms in water. If they have a little soil on them, simply brush it off with a dry paper towel. Cut them in half (or in quarters, if they're very large) and place them in a medium-size bowl. Drizzle the Olive Oil over the top, followed by the Lemon Juice and Basil. Stir well...adding a generous amount of Garlic Salt and freshly ground Pepper to taste. You'll want to OVER DO IT a little bit, as after they marinate for a few hours, the mushrooms will absorb much of the "zing" you taste at first. Place the mushrooms in a covered plastic container for several hours, or over night. Remove them from the refrigerator and allow them to come to room temperature before serving.

STORAGE INFORMATION: Store them in a covered plastic container for up to 2 days. Do not freeze.

PREPARATION TIME: 10 minutes

YIELD: Serves 6 to 8

13

POLPETTINE DI SPINACI
Deep Fried Spinach Balls

A tasty and popular hors d'oeuvre that will add excitement to your next gathering!

1 10-ounce package frozen Chopped Spinach
2 tablespoons Butter
2 slices coarse-grained Bread
¾ cup Milk
2 Whole Eggs
2 Egg Yolks
3 tablespoons grated Parmesan Cheese
Salt and Pepper to taste
Additional Bread Crumbs
Enough Vegetable Oil for deep frying

Defrost the chopped spinach by placing it in a collander under hot, running water. Squeeze as much water out of the spinach as you can, and saute it in the butter for 4 to 5 minutes. Remove it to a medium size bowl, and set it aside to cool. Meanwhile, soak the bread in the milk for about 10 minutes, or until nearly all the milk is absorbed. Squeeze it as dry as you can, and crumble it into the bowl with the spinach. In a smaller bowl, beat together the eggs, egg yolks and cheese, and combine them with the spinach mixture. Then add enough additional DRY bread crumbs to make the mixture firm enough to shape into 1" balls. Add salt and pepper to taste. After shaping, roll them in more bread crumbs and place them on a baking sheet lined with 2 layers of waxed paper and cover them with plastic wrap until a few minutes before serving time. In a deep fryer, or a heavy saucepan, heat 2 to 3 inches of good quality vegetable oil to approximately 375 degrees. (Using a candy thermometer to test the temperature works very well. But, if you don't have one, there's a method that's almost as good. Simply drop a 1" cube of fresh bread into the oil. If, at the end of 60 seconds, the bread is a deep, golden brown, the temperature is just right!) Drop the spinach balls into the oil, a few at a time. When they're lightly browned, remove them from the oil with a slotted spoon, and transfer them to paper towels to drain. Keep them hot in a preheated 250 degree oven until you're ready to serve them.

SPECIAL TIP: If you freeze the polpettine for future use, be sure to take them out of the freezer about 30 minutes before you intend to fry them, and let them come up to room temperature. That way, when you serve them, the centers will be nice and hot, too!

STORAGE INFORMATION: Store the uncooked polpettine in the refrigerator for up to a day ahead. If you like, freeze them on waxed paper-lined baking trays. Just gather them up after they're frozen and store them in a plastic bag. That way, they'll keep for up to 60 days!

PREPARATION TIME: 30 minutes

YIELD: Serves 6

GAMBERETTI ALL'OLIO E LIMONE
Marinated Shrimp

Prepare the marinade and the shrimp seperately and combine them just before serving! A stunning focal point for your antipasto!

1 pound of frozen Baby Shrimp (already cooked, peeled & deveined)
½ cup Extra Virgin Olive Oil
2 tablespoons fresh Lemon Juice
1 clove Garlic, minced
¼ teaspoon Salt
½ teaspoon Oregano

Defrost the shrimp by placing them in a collander, and running cold water over them. Drain them well and place them in a covered plastic container in the refrigerator. Meanwhile, in a small bowl, whisk together the remaining ingredients, and put that mixture in a seperate plastic container. About 30 minutes before serving time, combine the shrimp and the marinade and then serve.

SPECIAL TIP: Resist the temptation to combine the shrimp with the marinade ahead of time…it will make the shrimp tough!

STORAGE INFORMATION: Store in seperate containers until 30 minutes before serving time.

PREPARATION TIME: 15 minutes

YIELD: Serves 6

BASTONCINI DI PATATE CON FORMAGGIO
Cheese Stuffed Potato Croquettes

A tasty treat...with a surprise center of creamy melted cheese!

3 large Russet Potatoes
(about 1½ to 2 pounds...peeled and quartered)
3 Egg Yolks
3 tablespoons Butter, melted
¼ cup Bread Crumbs
¼ cup minced Fresh Onion
4 to 6 ounces Fontina (or Fontinella) Cheese
(Mozzarella, while quite different, works well, too!)
Salt and Pepper to taste
1 Whole Egg, beaten
More Bread Crumbs for coating
Vegetable Oil for deep frying

Cook the potatoes in salted boiling water until tender when pierced with a fork. Drain well and mash. Add the egg yolks, butter, minced onion, and the ¼ cup of bread crumbs. Mix thoroughly. Season with salt and pepper to taste. Set aside. Cut the cheese into strips approximately ¼" X ¼" X 2". Using about 2 tablespoons of the potato mixture, cover each strip of cheese forming a "sausage" shaped croquette. Dip each croquette into the beaten egg and roll it in bread crumbs. Set aside, until all the croquettes are ready. Heat the vegetable oil in a deep fryer (or other suitable pan), to 375 degrees, and fry the croquettes, a few at a time, until DEEP golden brown. Drain on paper towels and keep hot in a 200 degree oven until all the croquettes are ready. Serve hot.

SPECIAL TIP: Be sure to fry the croquettes until they are a DEEP golden brown...otherwise the cheese will not reach the proper melting temperature! Having them at room temperature before frying, helps!

STORAGE INFORMATION: Before deep frying, place the croquettes on waxed paper covered baking sheets and refrigerate until it's time to fry them. To keep them for future use, freeze them first, (uncooked) and then gather them up and place them in a plastic bag. Store them in the freezer for up to 60 days.

PREPARATION TIME: 1 hour.

YIELD: 6 to 8 servings

INVOLTINI DI MELANZANE
Eggplant Appetizers Stuffed With Parma Ham and Mozzarella

A unique recipe I adapted from one I saw in SALE E PEPE, the Italian food magazine whose name means "salt and pepper".

1 large, fresh Eggplant
Coarse Salt
3 ounces Prosciutto, sliced wafer thin
(boiled ham may be substituted, but the flavor is not the same)
4 to 6 ounces Mozzarella, cut into ¼" X ¼" X 2" sticks
Coarsely Ground Black Pepper
Enough Dry Bread Crumbs to coat (about ⅓ cup)
4 tablespoons Butter

Slice the eggplant into ⅛" rounds. (If you have one, a meat slicer works very well for this... if not, a thin, sharp butcher knife will do the trick!) Line a baking tray with paper towels, and sprinkle the surface of the towels with coarse salt. Put the eggplant rounds on top of the salt in a single layer, and sprinkle with more salt. Let the salted eggplant sit for at least 30 minutes. This will accomplish several things. First of all, it will help draw out the excess water as well as any bitterness, and in addition, it will soften the slices, making it easier to stuff them. Rinse the salt from the slices under cold running water, and pat them dry with paper towels. Lay them out on a clean, dry countertop, and top each slice with a slice of the ham, and then a stick of the mozzarella. Grind a little Black Pepper over each slice, then roll them up and fasten them with a toothpick. Roll each appetizer in bread crumbs and set them aside. Melt the butter in a large skillet over medium/high heat and saute the appetizers until the cheese is melted, and beginning to run out the ends. Oh, YUM! Serve warm.

STORAGE INFORMATION: These can be made up to several hours ahead, and kept, covered, in the refrigerator. Then, just saute and serve.

PREPARATION TIME: 45 minutes

YIELD: 4 servings

OLIVE MARINATE
Marinated Ripe Olives

Good quality Italian olives are often impossible to find! This marinated olive makes a flavorful and welcome addition to any appetizer plate.

1 large can whole, pitted Ripe Olives
½ cup Extra Virgin Olive Oil
⅓ cup Red Wine Vinegar
1 or 2 small dried Red Chili Peppers
2 cloves of fresh Garlic, crushed
½ teaspoon Salt
Freshly ground Black Pepper to taste

Drain the Olives and put them in a medium size bowl. Add the remaining ingredients and stir well. Put the olives in a jar with a lid and place them in the refrigerator for at least a week before serving.

STORAGE INFORMATION: These olives will keep refrigerated for up to 30 days.

PREPARATION TIME: 10 minutes

YIELD: Serves 6 to 8

PEPERONI CON TONNO
Sweet Cherry Peppers Stuffed with Tuna

Truly light and nutritious, this is a real "zinger" on an antipasto plate!

1 large jar Sweet Cherry Peppers
(with the pickling juices)
1 6½-ounce can of Solid Albacore Tuna packed in Spring Water

Drain the tuna, and discard the juice. Set aside. Drain the peppers, reserving the juice. With a sharp knife, cut off the tops of the peppers and remove the seeds and membrane. Turn the hollow peppers upside down onto paper towels, and allow to drain. Place a chunk of tuna into each pepper, and return it to the jar. When all of the peppers have been stuffed, fill the jar with the reserved pickling juice. Replace the lid on the jar, and refrigerate until needed. Serve chilled, or at room temperature.

STORAGE INFORMATION: Keeps well up to 1 week or more in the refrigerator.

PREPARATION TIME: 10-15 minutes

YIELD: 14 to 16 pieces

FUNGHI RIPIENI
Sausage Stuffed Mushrooms

An ideal treat to have in the freezer when friends drop by unexpectedly! Just pop them in the oven for a few minutes and TA-DAH!

20 to 24 large Mushrooms
(stems removed and set aside for another use)
1 to 1½ pounds Sweet Italian Sausage
(or Hot Italian Sausage, if you prefer)
½ cup Bread Crumbs
½ cup Heavy Whipping Cream
3 large Eggs, beaten lightly
½ cup grated Parmesan Cheese
½ teaspoon Thyme
1 teaspoon Basil
1 teaspoon Oregano
1 tablespoon Parsley
½ teaspoon Garlic Salt
½ teaspoon freshly ground Black Pepper
Additional Bread Crumbs
¼ pound (1 stick) Butter, melted

In a large skillet, brown the sausage and remove with a slotted spoon to a bowl lined with paper towels to remove the excess fat. Meanwhile, combine the cream and the bread crumbs, stirring well. Set aside for 15 to 20 minutes, or until all the cream is absorbed into the bread crumbs, making a thick "paste". In a large bowl, combine the browned meat, bread crumb "paste", eggs, cheese, herbs and spices…stir well. Add enough additional bread crumbs to make the mixture fairly firm. Dip the mushroom caps into the melted butter, shaking off any excess. Place the caps on a baking sheet hollow side up. Place about 1 rounded teaspoon of the meat mixture into each cap. Bake FUNGHI RIPIENI in a pre-heated 400 degree oven for about 20 minutes, or until lightly brown on top and bubbling. Serve hot.

SPECIAL TIPS: The measurements given for the herbs are for DRIED herbs. If FRESH herbs are used, you'll need to double the quantities shown. When herbs are dried, not only do they become smaller, and take up less space…but their flavors are intensified! Also, be aware that the reasonable shelf life for a dried leafy herb is only about 1 year.

STORAGE INFORMATION: If you are making these for future use, DO NOT BAKE, simply assemble as directed, and place them on a baking sheet lined with wax paper…cover and place in the freezer until frozen solid. Then, gather them up and put them in a freezer bag until you need them! Then bake for 30 mins.

PREPARATION TIME: 40 minutes

YIELD: 20 to 24 pieces

BURRO AL TONNO
Tuna Butter

Unbelievably simple...you'll find this spread disappearing off the hors d'oeuvre table! Spread it on thin slices of fresh French bread, and garnish with thin strips of fresh tomato and a few capers.

1 3/4-ounce can of Tuna packed in Oil (do not drain)
6 ounces of Butter (1½ sticks)
1 rounded teaspoon of Capers (drained)

Let butter soften to room temperature. (Depending on the temperature of the room...at least 1 hour) Place all the ingredients in a food processor fitted with a steel blade and process for 60 seconds, or until smooth.

STORAGE INFORMATION: Stores well in the refrigerator for up to 1 week.

PREPARATION TIME: Actual time 10 minutes (not including time to soften butter)

YIELD: About a cup of spread

INVOLTINI DI MANZO CON PROSCIUTTO
Grilled Flank Steak Stuffed with Parma Ham

If you're a beef lover...this one's for you!

1½ to 2 pounds Flank Steak
4 ounces thinly sliced Prosciutto
3 tablespoons Extra Virgin Olive Oil
1 teaspoon fresh Garlic, minced
Salt and freshly ground Black Pepper to taste

Slice the flank steak on the diagonal with a very sharp knife as thinly as you can manage. Lay the slices out on a countertop, and cover them with a thin piece of the prosciutto. Grate black pepper over all...roll them up and secure each one with a toothpick. Heat the oil and the garlic in a skillet large enough to hold all the roll-ups in a single layer. Add the beef and saute quickly over medium-high heat until the centers are medium-rare (3 to 5 minutes). Remove from the stove and place the roll-ups on a serving plate. Sprinkle with salt to suit your own tastes, and allow to rest for 5 minutes before serving. Serve warm.

SPECIAL TIPS: Don't salt the beef until you remove it from the heat. Salting before or during cooking will dry the steak out, and make it tough! Also...if you have the roll-ups at room temperature before you cook them, they don't take as long, and they will cook more evenly.

STORAGE INFORMATION: The roll-ups can be made up several hours in advance, covered wtih plastic wrap and stored in the refrigerator until a few minutes before serving time.

PREPARATION TIME: 15 minutes

YIELD: 4 servings

ZUCCHINE RIPIENE DI GAMBERETTI
Zucchine Rounds Stuffed with Baby Shrimp

One of our most popular appetizers, this was served on our 24th feast, in the Winter/Spring of 1989.

6 ounces frozen Baby Shrimp,
defrosted (the kind that are already cooked,
peeled and deveined are great for this recipe!)
1 Egg, seperated
1 clove Garlic, minced
1 teaspoon Dried Parsley Flakes
¼ cup Extra Virgin Olive Oil
1 tablespoon Bread Crumbs
Salt and Pepper to taste
2 medium to large Zucchine

Par boil the zucchine in a large pot (whole) for 5 to 7 minutes. Drain, and plunge into ice water to stop the cooking process. Set aside. Preheat oven to 400 degrees. Meanwhile, place the remaining ingredients (except the egg white) in the work bowl of a food processor. Pulse a few times to mix well, and coarsely chop the shrimp. BE CAREFUL NOT TO OVER PROCESS...you'll want nice size chunks of the shrimp...not a "puree"! Add salt and a dash of pepper to suit your own taste and set the shrimp mixture aside, while you prepare the zucchine. Slice the zucchine into ½ inch thick rounds. Then, using a melon baller, scoop out an indentation in the center of the round about ¼ inch deep. Place the rounds on an oiled baking tray. Lightly beat the egg white, and with a pastry brush, coat the indentation of each round. (The egg white will help hold the filling in place.) Place a rounded teaspoon of the shrimp mixture into each piece. Bake for 10 to 12 minutes. Serve immediately.

SPECIAL TIP: Zucchine tends to have a lot of excess moisture when cooked. Before coating with the egg white, blot the rounds with a paper towel.

STORAGE INFORMATION: The shrimp mixture can be made a day ahead and the zucchine stuffed just before baking.

PREPARATION TIME: 30 minutes

YIELD: 4 to 5 servings

Le Minestre

Soups

FETTUCINE AND THE SOUP TUREEN

Wilderness is the last true sanctuary of the Grizzly Bear, the Bald Eagle, the Magpie, and the Wolf—all endangered species. It is a sanctuary for several species that are not endangered . . . the Martin, Fisher, Mink, Bushy-tailed Wood Rat, Weasel, Vole, Shrew, and, the Deer Mouse . . . all with one thing in common . . . they belong to the rodent family.

When we first arrived to inspect the lodge, prior to making a decision to buy it, the first creatures whose calling cards were readily apparent were the Deer Mouse and his cousin, the Bushy-tailed Wood Rat . . . otherwise known as the Pack Rat.

We knew we had to convince these two critters that their place was outdoors . . . not inside. We began by setting live traps for the bushy-tailed ones, and the "snapping" variety for the mice. We had four live traps and seventeen mouse traps going at any one time.

By the time we were setting the seventeenth trap, the first one was snapping on its target. Some evenings it sounded like a string of fire crackers going off. The live traps were working very well since, unlike the mice who are constantly in love, the bushy-tailed pack rats only fall in love once a year.

Of course you know what happened to the mice in the traps,

but perhaps you are wondering what we did with the critters we caught in the live traps? We must confess they were released at various locations in the forest, alive and well. They are the natural food of Coyotes and Eagles, whom we consider our friends, and not nearly as plentiful as the mice. We also released a few at various other lodges we thought might be in short supply.

However, in no time at all, it became apparent we were losing our battle with the mice. So, we called in the world's most efficient eradicator . . . the cat!

We named our kitten gladiator "Fettucine". It didn't take him long to become the absolute reigning monarch of the lodge and grow to nearly twenty pounds on a diet of deer mice and a small handful of dry cat food per day.

Nevertheless, he couldn't keep up with the seasonal hordes that regularly invaded the area. We had to adopt his brother, (whom we named "Guido") who is deathly afraid of people. He hisses and bares his teeth as a defense mechanism.

Well, Fettucine and Guido had the run of the lodge building from freezer room to the front door on days we weren't serving the feast. Otherwise, they were confined to the freezer room. Fettucine followed Nancy and me wherever we went in the lodge, purring . . . talking to us, and asking to be petted. Guido remained hidden . . . coming out from various hiding places only when he heard us putting dry cat food in his bowl.

Favorite spots for both Fettucine and Guido are the sun filled windows. That's understandable, however, the lodge windowsills are barely three inches wide and the curtains extend below them. Also, near every window there are live plants, tables and stools with knickknacks, doodads, and antiques. Often we would have a bit of chaos when big fat Fettucine got clumsy. Guido is much more agile and has great equilibrium.

One morning we arrived at the lodge to find one window curtain on the floor, another hanging sideways off a single hook, and the big Ficus tree on the floor with its roots exposed among the pieces of the shattered pot. Fettucine was in hiding . . . a smart move, as Nancy was furious.

Three days later, with Nancy and Fettucine friends again, we were working in the kitchen when we heard a huge clatter from the dining room . . . crash, bang, thud, tinkle, tinkle and "Yeeooowl!", followed by Fettucine bolting thru the kitchen for the freezer room, all four feet skidding on the linoleum as he rounded the turns.

We rushed into the dining room, dreading what we would find. Sure enough, it was total destruction below the big front window at the table for six. Curtain down, rod bracket broken off, hanging plant swinging at a 45 degree angle from one string, lamp on the floor with the shade broken, antique bowl from Lebanon shattered. Worst of all, Nancy's precious soup tureen, ladle and lid, were all in pieces.

Nancy went for the broom. I knew it wasn't to sweep up the carpet, so I rushed to open the back door to provide Fettucine an escape route, so I wouldn't have to clean up pieces of a dead cat.

Today, Guido is the reigning monarch of the lodge.

Fettucine, banished forever to the outdoors, is alive and well . . . so long as he doesn't mess around in any of Nancy's herb gardens—for I have no way of stopping a speeding bullet!

VELLUTATA DI CARCIOFI CON POLPETTINE DI VITELLO
Cream of Artichoke Soup with Veal Meatballs

A memorable soup that, while taking it's origins from Northern Italy, was solely my invention. The combination of ingredients was so compelling...I couldn't help myself!

1 recipe VELLUTATA DI FUNGHI, substituting
1 8½-ounce can Artichoke Hearts (drained and chopped)
for the Mushrooms (all else remains the same)

For the meatballs:

1 pound Ground Veal
1 large Egg
2 teaspoons dried Basil
½ teaspoon Salt
¼ teaspoon White Pepper
½ teaspoon Garlic Powder
3 tablespoons   Bread Crumbs

Make the soup according to our recipe, substituting artichoke hearts for the mushrooms. Combine all the ingredients for the meatballs in a food processor fitted with a steel blade. Process for 1 minute, or until the meat is chopped very fine, and blended with the other ingredients. Shape the meat mixture into ½ inch to 1 inch balls and drop them (as you make them) into the simmering soup. Simmer for 30 to 40 minutes. Serve hot.

STORAGE INFORMATION: Store in a covered plastic container in the refrigerator for up to one week...in the freezer for up to 3 months.

PREPARATION TIME: 1½ hours (including cooking time)

YIELD: 1½ quarts

CIPOLLATA
Onion Soup

If you think the French are the only ones who know how to make delicious Onion Soup...you haven't tasted Cipollata!!! A light and delightful variation of the standard version, Cipollata originated in Umbria (in Central Italy), where they make the most of ALL root vegetables! Topped with freshly grated Parmesan Cheese, it rivals the finest "Onion Soup au Gratin" I've ever had...with an Italian difference!

6 Large White Onions (sliced EXTRA thin)
½ pound Pancetta (or Bacon, if Pancetta is unavailable)
(thinly sliced, then cut into short strips)
¼ cup Olive Oil
6 to 8 large fresh Tomatoes, peeled and diced
OR
1 28-ounce can of Whole Peeled Italian Style Tomatoes, chopped
1 ½ teaspoons dried Basil (or 3 teaspoons chopped fresh Basil)
¼ teaspoon freshly ground Black Pepper
¼ cup Chicken Flavored Soup Base (or more, if desired)
6 cups Water
Eggs and Parmesan Cheese (See "TO FINISH")

Soak the sliced onions overnight in cold water. (This will take away the "heat" of the onion!) Saute the pancetta (or bacon) in the olive oil in a large stock pot over medium heat, until the pancetta begins to brown. Add the onions and continue sauteing until they are limp and transluscent. Then add the tomatoes (including the juice), water, basil, pepper and soup base. (After the soup has simmered a while, you may want to "adjust" the flavor of the soup by adding more soup base, but BE CAREFUL...the soup base tends to be very salty, and a little goes a long way!) Stir and simmer for at least 1 hour. (As with most soups, the longer it simmers, the BETTER!) TO FINISH: Just before serving, stir in 1 beaten egg and 1 tablespoon of Parmesan cheese PER SERVING. Heat thoroughly, but DO NOT BOIL once the eggs have been added...otherwise the eggs will "curdle".

STORAGE INFORMATION: Soup that has not had the eggs and cheese added will freeze beautifully for up to 6 months! Just save out that portion you are not going to use the first time...and freeze it in a plastic container!

PREPARATION TIME: 1½ hours

YIELD: 8 1-cup servings

VELLUTATA DI CAROTE
Cream of Carrot Soup

This was a VERY popular soup with our guests. Perhaps the reason was that it was so unexpected! What sounded like a fairly boring soup, turned out to have an extraordinary flavor. The secret to the depth of the flavor, is that this soup is made like a "bisque". That is to say, you begin with a variety of vegetables, saute them in butter, cook them in broth until very soft, then puree them and add cream for body.

2 pounds fresh Carrots, peeled and shredded
2 cups fresh Celery, thinly sliced
1 large Onion, minced
1 28-ounce can Italian-style Pear Tomatoes, chopped
6 tablespoons Butter
2 quarts Chicken Broth
2 teaspoons ground Marjoram
¼ teaspoon ground White Pepper
Salt to taste
2 cups Heavy Whipping Cream

Saute the carrots, celery and onion in the butter in a large stock pot over medium heat until tender. Add the tomatoes (including the juice), the broth, the marjoram and white pepper. Simmer for at least 1 hour. Set off the heat and let cool. In a blender, puree the soup in batches, until it is all a smooth consistancy. Return it to the pot and add the cream. Heat thoroughly and taste. Add salt, as necessary. Serve hot. If you like, top the soup, as we did, with croutons.

STORAGE INFORMATION: Keeps well in a plastic container either in the refrigerator (for up to a week), or in the freezer for 3 months.

PREPARATION TIME: 2 hours

YIELD: 2 quarts

VELLUTATA DI FUNGHI
Cream of Mushroom Soup

A marvelous and very basic recipe, this can be adapted to your own favorite cream soup. Just substitute Broccoli, Celery, Cauliflower, Asparagus, Artichokes, etc., etc., etc., and you've got it made! (All else remains the same.)

6 tablespoons Butter
1 small Onion, minced
1 pound fresh Mushrooms, sliced
2 cups Chicken Broth
Dash of White Pepper
Dash of Nutmeg
½ cup Marsala wine, or Straight Sherry (optional)
3 cups Heavy Whipping Cream
Gold Medal Wondra to thicken
Salt and Pepper to taste

In a large stock pot, saute the onion in the butter over medium heat for 3 or 4 minutes, or until transparent. Then add the mushrooms and continue sauteing until the the mushrooms begin to lightly brown. (If you're using another type of vegetable, such as broccoli, saute just until tender, without browning.) Then add the chicken broth, white pepper, nutmeg and Marsala wine. Lower the heat and simmer for 30 to 40 minutes, stirring occasionally. Then add the whipping cream and bring the soup slowly to a boil. Thicken the soup as desired with the Gold Medal Wondra and adjust the seasoning with salt and pepper to your own taste.

STORAGE INFORMATION: This soup will keep in the freezer for up to 3 months, or in the refrigerator for 1 week.

PREPARATION TIME: 90 minutes

YIELD: About 5 cups

MINESTRA DI ANITRA
Duck Soup

A satisfying Winter soup…rich with cream, tender duck meat and root vegetables. What's not to love!?!?

1 whole Duck, cleaned
2 cups diced Turnips
2 cups diced Carrots
2 cups sliced Celery
1½ cup minced Onion
½ cup Chicken Flavored Soup Base
3 tablespoons chopped fresh Parsley (or 1½ tablespoons dried Parsley Flakes)
3 large Bay Leaves
Coarse Ground Black Pepper to taste
1 quart Heavy Whipping Cream
Enough Gold Medal Wondra to thicken as desired

The day before you'd like to serve the soup, place the duck in a large stock pot, cover with water and simmer (covered) for at least 2 hours, or until tender. Remove from heat and allow to cool. Refrigerate over night. The next morning, the excess fat from the duck will have solidified on the top of the broth. Remove and discard it. Take the duck from the broth and remove all fat, skin and bones. Reserve meat…chop and add to the broth, along with all but the last two ingredients, and simmer for at least 1 hour. Then add the cream and bring to a gentle boil. Thicken to the desired consistancy with Gold Medal Wondra. Serve hot.

STORAGE INFORMATION: This soup will keep in the refrigerator for up to 1 week, or in the freezer for up to 3 months.

PREPARATION TIME: Total of 3½ hours including cooking time.

YIELD: 3 quarts

MINESTRONE

A wonderfully simple recipe! If you like, top the soup bowls with freshly grated Parmesan Cheese and serve with garlic toast.

8 cups Water
1½ to 2 pounds meaty Beef Soup Bones
2 15-ounce cans Tomato Sauce with Bits
1 10-ounce package frozen Succotash
1 10-ounce package frozen Chopped Spinach
1 10-ounce package frozen Okra (sliced)
1 medium Onion, coarsely chopped
2 baking-size Russet Potatoes, diced
1 cup finely sliced Celery
2 Bay Leaves
1 tsp. dried Parsley (or 2 tsp. fresh Parsley, chopped)
1 tsp. dried Oregano (or 2 tsp. fresh Oregano, chopped)
½ tsp. Coarse Ground Black Pepper
½ cup Beef Soup Base
1 tsp. Salt
2 Tbsp. Worchestershire
¼ lb. Vermicelli, broken into small pieces

Combine all ingredients and simmer for 1 hour. Remove soup bones and remove any meat. Dice or shred it and return it to the soup. Serve while piping hot!

STORAGE INFORMATION: Will keep in the refrigerator for 1 week, or in the freezer for up to 3 months.

PREPARATION TIME: 90 minutes (including cooking time)

YIELD: About 3 quarts

ZUPPA VERDE CON POLPETTINE
Spinach Soup with Tiny Meatballs

One of our earliest soups…it is the only soup we ever repeated. It appeared again on our "pick hits" feast in December of 1985.

8 cups Water
⅓ cup Chicken Flavored Soup Base
1 10-ounce package frozen Chopped Spinach
1 recipe POLPETTE DI SALSICCIA
Grated Parmesan Cheese to garnish

Combine water, soup base and spinach in a large stock pot and bring to a boil. Reduce heat and simmer. Meanwhile, make the meatballs according to my recipe for POLPETTE DI SALSICCIA, but shape them into ½ inch balls, dropping them into the soup as you do. Let the soup simmer for 1 hour. Serve hot, garnished with a little grated Parmesan Cheese.

STORAGE INFORMATION: This soup keeps very well in the refrigerator for several days, or in the freezer for up to 3 months.

PREPARATION TIME: 1½ hours including simmering time.

YIELD: 2 quarts

Breads and Pastries

Il Pane e Pasticceria

FOCACCIA BALLET

There is at least one hazard in our business that does not exist in any other food serving operation.

We prepare every course fresh for the exact number of guests coming each evening. If I stumble on my way to serve the course, or Nancy drops a pan or tray, that course is over before it starts.

I do all the serving. When serving a table of six, I use a very large tray that will accommodate the entire course, not wanting anyone at the table to wait while I return to the kitchen for the rest of the guests' dishes. In the beginning I lived in fear of losing my balance, tripping over the different floor levels between the kitchen, lounge and dining rooms, and flinging the entire tray full into the middle of the table. That hasn't happened in six years, so shouldn't I relax? No, because some wag told me that each day that passes, that terrible day comes closer.

There was an evening, however, when, were it not for some extremely fancy footwork by both Nancy and me, one course was a goner.

On the evening in question, Nancy was preparing a special dish called Focaccia con Carciofi, (an Italian flat bread with an artichoke and cheese mixture on top), which she finished under the broiler. We had a full house that evening, so she was using the spare oven in the freezer room, as well as the kitchen oven.

We have a couple of topnotch mouser-cats, named Fettucine and Guido, who are restricted to the freezer room on days we are open. Even tho they are brothers, they have opposite personalities. Fettucine is an unabashed total extrovert who loves all humans. He especially makes up to folks he perceives as pushovers for loud purring and leg rubs. Guido is so introverted and terrified of humans that, even when we approach him, he shrinks into a corner, bares his teeth and hisses . . . a totally defensive gesture, as he then loves for us to pet and stroke him.

Nancy took the full tray of focaccia from under the broiler, balancing the tray on one hand while closing the oven door with the other, turned toward the kitchen just as Fettucine made his move to rub her ankles with tail in the air.

Nancy tripped over Fettucine, and, whirling in a circle trying to regain her balance, the tray tipped up sideways and all the focaccia started to slide off the tray. In an instant she regained her balance and saw the only hope of saving the course was to plaster the whole tray against the face of the freezer door.

Returning from the dining room, I heard Nancy calling "Help! Help!" from the freezer room. I ran to the door and opened it to find Nancy sinking to her knees with the tray of focaccia sliding lower and lower down the freezer door as she tried to keep any of the portions from escaping.

I ran back to the kitchen, grabbed the big spatula and an empty tray, and raced back to Nancy. As she tilted the tray away from the face of the door, I carefully scraped each portion of focaccia off the door and placed them on the empty tray. Nancy redressed them with extra artichoke spread and placed them back under the broiler.

If memory serves me correctly—I believe that was the last time we ever used that oven!

NOTE: For the recipe, combine Focaccia All 'Olio e Sale (Italian Flat Bread with Olive Oil and Salt) with Carciofi e Formaggio al Forno (Baked Artichoke Spread with Cheese) . . . but we DON'T recommend plastering them against the freezer door before serving!

PANE TOSCANO
Tuscan Bread

Few breads are as quick and easy to make as this one...and yet so-o-o-o-o satisfying! The fact that it only requires ONE rising is a real time-saver!

2 tablespoons Active Dry Yeast
4 cups Water (at 105 to 110 degrees)
5 cups White Flour
2 cups Whole Wheat Flour
2 tablespoons Sugar
1 teaspoon Salt
Enough extra White flour to finish the dough
Corn Meal
3 tablespoons Butter, melted

Dissolve the yeast in the warm water, and set aside while you combine the next four ingredients. Then add the water/yeast mixture, and mix well. Turn out onto a clean, dry counter-top sprinkled with some flour, and add enough extra flour while kneading, to make the dough dry enough so as to not be sticky to the touch. (It will take a cup or more!) Knead until smooth and elastic...about 10 minutes. Cut the dough in half and shape into 2 round loaves. Place loaves on cookie sheets that have been sprinkled with corn meal. Cover with a clean towel and place in a warm draft-free place to rise (about 1 hour) until double. Preheat oven to 400 degrees. Brush the loaves with melted butter, then slash the tops with a very sharp knife and bake for 30 to 40 minutes, or until they sound hollow when tapped with your finger. Place finished loaves on cake racks and cover with towels to cool. Great with almost any meal...but this versatile bread makes fabulous sandwiches and incredible toast! When the bread is a few days old, try PANZANELLA (Tuscan Bread Salad)!

STORAGE INFORMATION: As soon as bread is cooled, place in a plastic bag and refrigerate (for 3 or 4 days) or freeze (for up to 1 month).

PREPARATION TIME: 1½ to 2 hours...start to finish.

YIELD: Makes 2 large Loaves

PANE SICILIANO
Sicilian Rolls with Prosciutto and Parmesan Cheese

A savory dinner roll with bits of Parma Ham and Onions...topped with melted Parmesan cheese! A fabulous addition to a meal of VITELLO FARCITO.

3 tablespoons Active Dry Yeast
1 tablespoon Sugar
1 cup Warm Water (at 100 to 105 degrees)
4 tablespoons Butter, cut into small pieces
¾ cup Hot Water (at 115 degrees or more)
2 teaspoons Salt
5 to 6 cups Unbleached White Flour
1 small Onion, minced
2 tablespoons Butter
4 ounces Prociutto, minced
Cornmeal
1 Egg White, beaten
⅓ cup grated Parmesan Cheese

In a small bowl, combine the yeast, sugar and warm water. Let stand for five minutes, or until bubbly. Meanwhile, combine the hot water, salt, and the 4 tablespoons of butter...melting the butter. Let cool. Saute the onion in the two tablespoons of butter and set aside. Combine the butter/water and yeast/water mixtures and add the flour, one cup at a time, mixing well after each addition. Turn the dough out onto a clean, dry counter and add the sauteed onion and minced prosciutto. Knead well for 10 minutes, adding just enough flour to keep the dough from being sticky. Divide the dough into ping-pong-size balls, and nestle them into three lightly buttered cake pans. Preheat the oven to 425 degrees. Let the rolls rise in a warm place for 30 to 40 minutes, or until double in size. Brush lightly with the beaten egg white. Bake for about 15 minutes, and then sprinkle them with the grated cheese and return them to the oven for another 10 minutes, or until a deep golden brown. Serve hot.

SPECIAL TIP: Just bake the number of rolls you need to accompany your meal (2 to 4 per person), and freeze the rest right in the cake pans!

STORAGE INFORMATION: You can freeze the unbaked rolls for up to 1 month. When you want to serve them...just defrost them and let them come up to room temperature and rise...then bake as usual!

PREPARATION TIME: 1½ hours

YIELD: 36 small rolls

FOCACCIA ALL'OLIO E SALE
Italian Flat Bread with Olive Oil and Coarse Salt

This recipe is an adaptation of one that my friend Franca Facchetti was kind enough to share with me. She served them to me one day while in her home for an Italian lesson, and I nearly ate the entire batch myself! While you can use regular tap water, she tells me that the secret to this recipe is using bottled spring water! At the lodge, we have spring water "on tap"...so ours have always turned our perfectly!

2 cups Water (at 100 to 105 degrees)
1 teaspoon Sugar
2 teaspoons Salt
2 tablespoons Active Dry Yeast
3 cups Unbleached Flour (Plus enough extra flour to finish...about 1 cup)
Enough Extra Virgin Olive Oil to coat 16 Focaccia (about 1 cup)
Coarse Salt for topping (about 1 to 2 tablespoons) (Sea Salt or Kosher Salt)

Sprinkle the sugar and the yeast over the lukewarm water. Let stand until bubbly...about 5 minutes. In a large bowl, combine the salt and the flour...then add the yeast mixture and mix well. Turn out onto a clean, dry counter and knead well until smooth and elastic...adding enough additional flour to keep the dough from being sticky. Place the dough in an oiled bowl, turning to coat the top. Cover with a towel, and place the bowl in a warm place, until the dough is double in size...about 1 hour. Punch the dough down and knead the air bubbles out of it. Then shape it into an oblong, and beat it with a heavy rolling pin. (Franca says not to feel sorry for the dough...the end result is what's important!) Repeat this procedure for about 10 minutes, turning the dough frequently and, holding it by one end, slamming it on the counter...then beating it with the rolling pin again. It is properly kneaded, when an indentation made with your finger-tip springs right back. Divide the dough into 16 pieces and flatten them into 4" rounds with your finger-tips. Lightly oil 2 baking sheets, sprinkle with a little of the coarse salt and arrange the focaccia on them...8 per tray. Let rest 5 minutes, then, using your fingers, make 3 or 4 indentations in each focaccia. Brush the focaccia liberally with olive oil and sprinkle with more salt. Cover and let rise for 20 to 30 minutes. Meanwhile preheat oven to 425 degrees. Just before baking, pierce the focaccia in several places with a very sharp knife. Bake for 15 minutes, or until light golden brown.

SPECIAL TIP: Enhance the flavor of the salt by crushing it in a mortar and pestle, or rolling an empty wine bottle over it before including it in your recipe.

STORAGE INFORMATION: Store in an airtight container for 3 or 4 days, or in the freezer for up to one month.

PREPARATION TIME: 2 hours

YIELD: 16

PASTA FROLLA I
Sweet Egg Pastry

There are many ways to fill this lovely pastry...one of the best is a desert we've included in this book called CROSTATA ALLA CREMA! You can also bake the shell in advance, and make a sort of "fruit pizza" by filling it with Mascarpone (Italian cream cheese) and topping it with sliced fresh fruit!

1¾ cup Flour
⅓ cup Sugar
Pinch of Salt
12 ounces Butter (1½ sticks)
1 Whole Egg
1 Egg Yolk
1 teaspoon Vanilla
1 teaspoon Lemon Juice
Approximately 2 tablespoons Cold Water

Place the flour, sugar, salt and butter in the work bowl of a food processor fitted with a steel blade. Process until it is the consistancy of coarse meal. Combine the whole egg, the egg yolk, vanilla and lemon juice in a small bowl, and whisk with a wire whip until frothy. With the food processor running, add the egg mixture to the flour mixture. Drizzle the water into the feed tube 1 tablespoon at a time, (pulsing the machine) until the mixture begins to cling together. Do not over process. Distribute the dough evenly over the bottom of a tart or quiche pan...pressing it into shape, following the contours of the pan. An easy way to make the crust more even, is to top the dough with a sheet of plastic wrap while you're working. That way, it won't stick to your fingers, and you'll be able to get the surface smooth. Cover the unbaked crust with plastic wrap, and store it in the refrigerator while you make the filling.

VARIATION: If you wish to bake the crust in advance, place a sheet of aluminum foil on top of the tart, and press it into shape, following the contours of the pan. Fill the foil with "pie weights"...either the commercial variety, or use dried beans or uncooked rice. Bake in a preheated 375 degree oven for 25 to 30 minutes. About mid-way thru, remove the foil and finish the baking. This will insure that the shell holds its' shape, and will allow it to brown evenly. Let cool to room temperature before filling.

STORAGE INFORMATION: Bake and serve immediately.

PREPARATION TIME: 45 minutes
YIELD: 1 large Tart Shell

PASTA FROLLA II
Pastry for Savory Tarts

A quick and easy pastry crust you make in a food processor!

3 cups All Purpose Flour
¾ cup chilled Butter
Pinch of Salt
2 large Eggs
Cold Water
1 Whole Egg, beaten

Place the flour, butter and salt in the work bowl of a food processor fitted with a steel blade. Pulse the machine until the mixture resembles coarse meal. With the machine running, add the whole eggs, one at a time...and then a tablespoon or two of the cold water. When the dough begins to come together, stop the machine, and test the moisture content of the dough. The dough should be evenly moist...not soggy...not dry and crumbly! Gather the dough into a ball. DO NOT KNEAD THE DOUGH ANY MORE THAN IS NECESSARY TO SHAPE IT INTO A BALL. Cut the dough into two pieces...one slightly larger than the other, and proceed with your recipe...such as mine for CROSTATA RIPIENA DI BROC-COLI E RICOTTA. After the filling is added, and the top crust is in place and the edge sealed, brush the top of the pie with beaten egg...prick the top with a fork or a sharp knife...and bake.

STORAGE INFORMATION: Make the dough and fill the pie (up to several hours in advance)...then cover with plastic wrap and store in the refrigerator until you are ready to bake it...up to 4 hours.

PREPARATION TIME: 15 minutes for the crust itself (excluding baking time)

YIELD: 1 Two-Crust Pastry

GRISSINI
Bread Sticks

Well...here it is! THE recipe that so many of you have asked for...our "world famous" GRISSINI! You'll learn...to your surprise...that it is a very simple recipe...but, oh the finished product! One of the reasons they are so easy, is that you just make the dough...shape it into bread sticks...let it rise and BAKE! Only one rising cuts your time in half! A tradition at Brannon's...this is the recipe we served from the day we opened our doors!

4½ to 5 cups All Purpose Flour
3 tablespoons Active Dry Yeast
1 tablespoon Sugar
1 teaspoon Salt
¼ cup Extra Virgin Olive Oil
1½ cups Warm Water (at 110 to 115 degrees)
About 1 cup of additional Extra Virgin Olive Oil,
(or enough to coat 24 grissini)
1 beaten Egg White
Coarse Salt, Sesame and Poppy Seeds

Combine 2 cups of the flour in a large mixing bowl with the yeast, sugar, salt and olive oil. Add the water all at once and blend well with an electric mixer. (I use a Kitchen-Aid Mixer which is really wonderful. But, I have never liked the dough hook. I use the standard beater and mix everything really well while it's still fairly "liquid".) Then add the rest of the flour...turn it out onto the countertop and knead it by hand for about 10 minutes...adding a little more flour as needed to reach the proper consistancy. (The dough should be smooth and elastic, without being sticky.) Divide the dough into four equal parts...and then divide each of those into six equal parts. That way, you'll end up with 24 grissini just about the same size. Roll out each lump of dough to about the diameter of your little finger. Dip each one into olive oil...allowing the excess to drip off...and place it on a non-stick baking tray. (It's a good idea to wipe your hands well after each bread stick...otherwise, it makes the next one difficult to shape.) Each 11 X 17 inch baking tray will comfortably hold 12 grissini. When you have them all shaped, use a pastry brush and coat each grissini well with the beaten egg white, then sprinkle with your favorite toppings...coarse salt, sesame seeds or poppy seeds. If it's a warm day and the grissini are rising too fast for you to get all 24 shaped and coated, just place the first tray in the freezer until you're finished with the second tray. (A trick I've learned, is to wait until the grissini are slightly defrosted before coating them with the egg white and the toppings. If you try to do it while they are still frozen, the toppings will just slide off!) Then place both trays (uncovered) on the counter top, coat them as usual, and allow them to rise. Bake the grissini in a pre-heated 425 degree oven for about 15 to 20 minutes, or until they are lightly browned. (NOTE: You may want to seperate the grissini with a spatula about mid-way thru the baking time, to allow the edges to brown slightly, too. If they are soft, the grissini will break in half when you place them in a crock to serve them!) If you like, serve them hot, as we did, with Pesto Butter (see PESTO ALLA GENOVESE).

SPECIAL TIP: So as to make things easier the evening of your dinner, freeze the grissini coated with the olive oil on the trays up to 2 days ahead... covered with plastic wrap. Just coat them with the egg white and the toppings after you take them out of the freezer. Then allow them to defrost and rise...and bake them as usual.

STORAGE INFORMATION: The frozen grissini dough can be placed in a plastic bag and frozen BEFORE shaping. (You might only want to make 12 grissini...and freeze the other half of the dough for later!) Just defrost the dough and proceed to shape, coat and bake as ususal. Keeps 2 weeks in the freezer.

PREPARATION TIME: 1 hour

YIELD: 24

GRISSINI AL FINOCCHIO
Bread Sticks with Fennel

An unusual grissini made with BEER and seasoned with fennel! These are quite different from the traditional grissini served at Brannon's...these baked longer, in a slower oven, and are quite crispy! Because they are served at room temperature, they can be made up ahead, and stored in an airtight container until serving time.

1 tablespoon Active Dry Yeast (1 package)
¾ cup Warm Water (at 105 to 110 degrees)
½ cup Extra Virgin Olive Oil
¾ cup Dark Beer (at room temperature)
1 teaspoon Salt
1 tablespoon Fennel Seeds
5½ to 6 cups All Purpose Flour
1 Whole Egg, beaten with 1 tablespoon Water

In a large bowl, combine water and yeast. Set aside for 5 minutes, until softened. Add the olive oil, beer, salt and fennel seeds...stir well. With a heavy-duty mixer, or a large spoon, stir in 3 cups of the flour, until well blended. Add the remaining flour, and turn the mixture out onto a clean, dry countertop. Knead about 10 minutes, (adding more flour as needed to keep the dough from being sticky) until the dough forms a smooth ball. Place the dough in an oiled bowl...turning to coat the outside. Cover with a clean cloth, and allow to rise in a warm place until double in size (about 1 hour). Punch the dough down, and knead well to expell all of the air bubbles and give the dough a smooth texture. Pinch off balls of the dough about 1 inch in diameter and roll them into pencil-thin strips about 12 inches long. Place them, one at a time, onto an oiled baking tray and brush them with the beaten egg mixture. Bake the grissini in a pre-heated 350 degree oven for about 45 minutes, or until evenly brown and crisp. Cool on wire racks. Serve at room temperature.

SPECIAL TIP: To increase the flavor of the fennel, crush it in a mortar and pestle first!

STORAGE INFORMATION: Store in an airtight container for up to two weeks.

PREPARATION TIME: 2½ hours

YIELD: 48

Le Salse

Sauces

VEST POCKET BECHAMEL

Nancy and I have been cooking all our lives . . . Nancy, from the time she was big enough for her grandmother to stand her on a stool in front of the stove and let Nancy stir. She was four years old.

When I was seven, my father let me mix his famous flapjacks. He had all the ingredients ready, and let me put them in the bowl and stir, as he measured. The only thing he wouldn't let me do, was separate the eggs and beat the whites.

Our love of food and cooking was one of the major elements of our courtship. I know it is a binding force, in both our marriage and our partnership.

We have no employees . . . by choice. The evening, from start to finish, we want to be completely personal, yet private. We strive to marry the two concepts of fine dining . . . the host-guest relationship you enjoy in your own home, with the arms length "we will not intrude" atmosphere you expect in the finest restaurants. It is a very fine line.

And so it is in the kitchen. Each has a sphere of work responsibility . . . Nancy cooks and I serve . . . and it has become very similar to dancing. Each has learned when and where the other will be at any given moment, and, when everything is going smoothly, it's very much the same as a symphony, if you please. On the other hand, when it isn't going smoothly . . . well, you be the Judge.

In our kitchen, the stove and sink are side by side. More often than not . . . since Nancy cooks and I serve . . . we are also side by side.

This was one of those rare and exhilarating evenings in our first year of business, when we had four tables filled . . . just enough to pay the electric bill before they turned off our lights.

Nancy had placed in the rarebit dishes a fabulous lasagna, "Timbalo di Lasagna alla Modenese", and needed only to ladle the bechamel sauce over each dish, followed with a sprinkling of fresh parsley flakes.

She decided, in that moment of special ecstasy, to balance the tray of rarebit dishes, filled with lasagna, on one hand, while she ladled the bechamel sauce with the other, then whirl back to where she started, for the parsley. Ah, would that she were successful!

Standing at the sink, I hear Nancy cry out "Oh No!" and immediately I get hit in the left side, from vest pocket to shoelace, with lasagna and bechamel sauce . . . no fresh parsley flakes, of course, she hadn't gotten that far!

We looked at each other . . . I, in disbelief, as the gooey concoction slowly made its way down my vest and pant leg and plopped onto my shoe tops . . . Nancy with a combination of horror, embarrassment, and panic.

While I raced over to the chalet to change clothes, Nancy cleaned up the mess and sliced up Saturday's lasagna to serve the Friday evening.

By the time I returned, Nancy had the lasagna finishing in the oven. Smiling and visiting with our guests, pouring more wine, changing the music, and adding more wood to the fire, we were able to fill the time lag.

The rest of the feast went on without a single guest discovering the catastrophe in the kitchen. In fact, we received several compliments on the lasagna . . . and not one question as to why I was wearing different clothes!

SALSA DI SENAPE
Mustard Sauce

This versatile sauce keeps up to two weeks in the refrigerator and has many, many uses!

1 8-ounce jar DiJon-type Mustard
2 tablespoons minced fresh Onion
(dehydrated minced onion can be substituted here,
but the flavor is not nearly so nice!)
¼ cup Honey

Combine all ingredients. Serve.

SERVING SUGGESTIONS: Use as an accompaniment for slices of cold roast pork (see MAIALE ARROSTO AFFETATO) or beef...a dip for fresh vegetables...a spread to jazz up a ham sandwich...use your imagination!

SPECIAL TIP: If the honey seems a little stiff, just place the container in a bowl of hot water for a few minutes, and it will pour a lot easier! If the honey is actually beginning to crystalize, place the container in a pan of hot water and put it on the stove on low for a few minutes, stirring periodically, until smooth.

STORAGE INFORMATION: Store covered in a plastic container in the refrigerator for up to two weeks. Do not freeze.

PREPARATION TIME: 10 minutes.

YIELD: About 1 cup

PESTO ALLA GENOVESE
Fresh Basil Pesto

Fresh Basil is the key ingredient in this fabulous and versatile sauce! If you can't get fresh basil...wait until you CAN to make it!

2 cups fresh Basil Leaves (washed and patted dry)
½ cup freshly grated Parmesan Cheese
3 to 4 cloves fresh Garlic
1 teaspoon Coarse Salt
1 tablespoon Pignoli (Pine Nuts)
½ cup fresh Parsley (Flat Leafed Italian Parsley preferred)
¾ cup Extra Virgin Olive Oil

Place all of the ingredients in the work bowl of a food processor or blender. Process by pulsing the machine until all the ingredients are finely chopped...but not pureed...do not over-process!

SERVING SUGGESTIONS: Warm the sauce in a small skillet and toss with hot, fresh pasta, topped with a sprinkling of freshly grated Parmesan Cheese. Also...to mix ¼ cup of PESTO ALLA GENOVESE with 1 pound of butter (softened) and presto! You have PESTO BUTTER...just like we have served with our famous GRISSINI since we opened our doors!

SPECIAL TIP: Regardless of the time of year, even the dead of winter, don't give up on FRESH basil! Often a request to the Produce Manager of your favorite supermarket will produce fresh basil from his gourmet supplier down south!!

STORAGE INFORMATION: Keeps well in the refrigerator for a few days, or place in a plastic container...pour a thin layer of olive oil over the top...cover with a snug lid and place in the freezer. Keeps very well frozen for up to 1 year!

PREPARATION TIME: 20 minutes.

YIELD: About 1¼ cups

MAIONESE AL LIMONE
Lemon Mayonnaise

Don't be intimidated by those who try to tell you that making fresh mayonnaise is tricky! With this quick and easy method, you may never buy "store-bought" mayonnaise again!

1 large Egg (at room temperature)
¼ teaspoon Coarse Salt
¾ cup Extra Virgin Olive Oil
(either a mild or fruity one, at your pleasure!)
Juice of ½ Lemon (about 1½ tablespoons)

Combine the egg, salt and 3 tablespoons of the olive oil in a small bowl, or a blender. If you don't have a blender, a wire whisk will do nicely! Blend these ingredients until pale yellow and creamy. With the blender running (or while you're whisking), pour in the remaining oil in a thin, steady stream. (Stop pouring only if the oil is NOT being incorporated. Then blend until all the excess oil is absorbed...and then continue adding the remainder of the oil.) Finally, add the lemon juice all at once, and blend briefly to a smooth consistency.

VARIATIONS: For an unusual taste treat, flavor your mayonnaise with various herbs, such as tarragon...or perhaps a tablespoon of PESTO ALLA GENOVESE.

STORAGE INFORMATION: Place in a plastic or glass container with a snug lid (no metal, of course!) and refrigerate for up to 1 week. (Unfortunately, mayonnaise will not freeze.)

PREPARATION TIME: 10 minutes

YIELD: 1 cup

BALSAMELLA
Bechamel Sauce

A very basic sauce, so versatile, you'll want to keep some on hand all the time!

2 tablespoons Butter
1 cup Heavy Whipping Cream
Dash of Nutmeg
Dash of finely ground White Pepper
Enough Gold Medal Wondra to thicken as desired
Salt to taste

In a medium skillet, melt the butter. Add all the remaining ingredients except the Gold Medal Wondra. Bring the mixture to a boil over medium heat, stirring with a wire whisk. When the sauce is boiling, add a few sprinkles of Gold Medal Wondra, whisking it rapidly. Allow it to boil for a moment or two more to thicken. If the sauce is not as thick as you would like, add a little more Wondra, until the desired consistancy is reached.

SPECIAL TIP: If you reserve this sauce for future use, either in the refrigerator or freezer, it may tend to seperate when it is reheated. DON'T PANIC! Just warm it over low heat and whisk it with a wire whip. Suddenly...magically...it will come back together into creamy perfection!

STORAGE INFORMATION: Store in the refrigerator for up to 1 week, or in the freezer for up to 60 days.

PREPARATION TIME: 15 minutes

YIELD: About 1 cup

SALSA ALFREDO
Alfredo Sauce

The original Alfredo Sauce was invented by a creative restauranteur in Rome and became the basis for the now famous dish "Fettucine Alfredo". While Alfredo made the sauce right in the pan along with the pasta, we make the sauce seperately, so that you can use it right away, or store it for future use. With the use of a 36 to 40 percent butter fat cream, there is no problem with bringing the sauce to a full boil, thus enabling you to "reduce" the sauce to the desired thickness, and eliminate the need for using flour and butter to make a "roux".

1 cup Heavy Whipping Cream
3 tablespoons Butter
½ cup freshly grated Parmesan Cheese
Salt and Pepper to taste
Pinch of Nutmeg

Place the cream and butter in a skillet and bring to a full boil over medium heat. Continue to boil gently until sauce is reduced to the desired thickness (about 20 minutes). Using a wire whisk, stir in the cheese, and combine throughly. Then, add the nutmeg, and salt and pepper to taste. Keep hot until ready to serve.

SERVING SUGGESTION: Toss with hot fettucine (preferably home made...see BASIC EGG PASTA) and top with additional cheese and a sprinkling of chopped, fresh parsley. Serve as an accompaniment to meat, fish or fowl, or as a vegetarian entree.

STORAGE INFORMATION: Keep up to 1 week in the refrigerator, or 1 month in the freezer, in a covered container.

PREPARATION TIME: 30 minutes.

YIELD: About 1 cup

BAGNA CAUDA
Hot Anchovy and Garlic Sauce

From the famous Piedmont Region in Northern Italy, this sauce is primarily used as a dip for fresh vegetables...frequently served as a prelude to a fine dinner...or as a snack after skiing! You'll also find a recipe called INSALATA DI CAVOLO ROSSO ALLA TORINESE in this book...a red cabbage "slaw" of sorts (from the town of Turin in the Piedmont Region) that uses this wonderful recipe as it's dressing. How ever you serve it, you'll be amazed at how quickly your guests will become addicted to it!

½ cup Extra Virgin Olive Oil
2 tablespoons Butter
1 2-ounce can Flat Anchovy Filets
1 or 2 cloves of Garlic, minced (about a teaspoon)
1 tablespoon Heavy Cream

Combine all the ingredients in a small, heavy sauce pan (a heat-proof crockery one is ideal). Place it on the stove over medium heat. As the ingredients begin to melt, whisk the sauce with a wire whip until it is thick and creamy...bringing just to a simmer. Serve immediately.

SPECIAL TIP: Have everything else ready before you heat the Bagna Cauda, because you'll want to serve it very hot, and it does not re-heat well. I suggest placing all the ingredients in the pan first and setting it aside. Then prepare the vegetables and set the table. When everyone is seated, heat the Bagna Cauda...it only takes a couple of minutes!

STORAGE INFORMATION: Make up the sauce as much as a day ahead (without heating) and store it (covered) in the refrigerator until you are ready to heat and serve.

PREPARATION TIME: 5 to 10 minutes

YIELD: About ¾ cup

SALSA TONNATA
Tuna Sauce

A very traditional sauce from the Lombardy region, Salsa Tonnato dresses up almost any roast meat, and is extremely quick and easy to make! Make it a day or two ahead, and put it in a covered plastic container until mealtime! It is served cold, or nearly room temperature, and makes a tangy addition to any picnic! Now, don't cheat and leave out the Anchovies!...you'll be amazed at the difference in the flavor!

1 12½-ounce can Tuna packed in oil
¾ cup Extra Virgin Olive Oil
½ cup fresh Lemon Juice
(or the natural strength bottled juice will do!)
1 can Flat Anchovy Filets

Place all the ingredients in a blender or food processor and pulse off and on for a few seconds, or until a creamy consistency is reached, scraping down the sides from time to time with a rubber spatula. The traditional way to serve this sauce , is as a topping for tender slices of roast veal...however, a nice variation is to substitute slices of boneless, skinless breast of chicken, turkey, or roast pork. Line a platter with crisp lettuce leaves...arrange the meat slices in an attractive pattern and spoon the sauce down the center. Garnish with capers, if you like.

STORAGE INFORMATION: May be made a day or two ahead and stored in a covered plastic container until serving time. Do not freeze.

PREPARATION TIME: 10 minutes.

YIELD: About 2 cups

SALSA DI POMODORO
Tomato Sauce

This is an adaptation of a very traditional recipe from Sicily and parts of Southern Italy...sometimes called "Marinara Sauce" or "Pizzaola". We have served it many times on the feasts at the lodge...over pasta, steak, on pizza, and in lasagna!

2 28-ounce cans Italian-style Pear Tomatoes
1 12-ounce can Tomato Paste
1 medium Onion, minced
3 cloves Garlic, minced (about 1½ to 2 teaspoons)
⅓ cup Extra Virgin Olive Oil
1 tablespoon dried Oregano*
1 tablespoon dried Basil*
1 tablespoon dried Parsley*
½ teaspoon freshly ground Black Pepper
¼ cup Beef Flavored Soup Base
1 cup Dry Red Wine (a Chianti is ideal for this!)
Additional salt to taste

*Certainly, FRESH HERBS are preferred here . . . but may be hard
to find, depending on your location. If you are fortunate
enough to get them, just DOUBLE the quantities
listed here for dried herbs.

Drain the tomatoes, reserving the juice. Chop them coarsely, and set them aside. In a large sauce pan on medium heat, saute the onion in the olive oil until it begins to lightly brown. Then add the garlic, and saute a few moments more. Add the tomatoes and the reserved juice along with the remaining ingredients plus 1½ cups of water. Simmer for at least 2 hours, stirring frequently to avoid sticking, while reducing the sauce to a luscious thickness. Taste the sauce and add additional salt if needed. (The Beef Flavored Soup Base is quite salty, so you may not need any salt at all!)

VARIATION: Add a can of Flat Anchovy Filets (drained and chopped) and a tablespoon of capers (also drained and chopped) in place of the Beef Flavored Soup Base.

SPECIAL TIP: Aluminum pans tend to react to tomato sauces. By that I mean, they will give the sauce a metalic taste, which doctors are now discovering may not be good for you. Stainless steel pans are much better...but in any case, as soon as the sauce is finished, it should be placed in a non-reactive container, such as a glass or plastic one.

STORAGE INFORMATION: This sauce will keep well in the refrigerator for up to a week, or in the freezer for at least 6 months! I suggest dividing it up among several small plastic containers, so that you can defrost just the amount you'll need.

PREPARATION TIME: 2½ to 3 hours

YIELD: About 2 quarts

SALSA DI POMODORI FRESCHI
Fresh Tomato Sauce

Unlike the heavier tomato sauces found in Sicily and Southern Italy, this sauce from the Piedmont Region is quick and easy to prepare and has the unmistakable flavor of fresh garden goodies!

2 tablespoons Butter
2 tablespoons Extra Virgin Olive Oil
½ cup thinly sliced Celery
½ cup thinly sliced Onion
1 large Carrot, peeled and shredded
2 cloves fresh Garlic, minced
2 tablespoons fresh Basil, minced
(or 1 tablespoon dried Basil)
2 tablespoons fresh Parsley, minced
(or 1 tablespoon dried Parsley Flakes)
6 large ripe Tomatoes, diced
1 cup Dry White Wine
Salt and Pepper to taste

Over medium heat, saute celery, onion, carrot and garlic in butter and olive oil until limp, but not brown. Add basil and parsley and continue sauteing for 2 to 3 minutes. Add tomatoes and white wine, and simmer 20 to 30 minutes, until sauce begins to take on more "body"...adding salt and pepper to taste. Place atop a bed of homemade pasta (see BASIC EGG PASTA).

VARIATIONS: Place steamed shrimp atop the pasta first, and then top with the sauce!

STORAGE INFORMATION: May be kept in the refrigerator in a covered container for up to 1 week or in the freezer for 3 months.

PREPARATION TIME: 45 minutes

YIELD: 4 to 6 servings

I Piatti Principali

Main Courses

WOOTSEE AND THE MOOSE

When we first came into the wilderness, to restore this old lodge, we had a little indoor dog named "Wootsee" . . . the term Nancy's best friend uses for anything very small.

Wootsee was almost all black with just some white chin whiskers and a small patch of white on his chest. His heritage was in question, tho apparently a Scotty had visited the family somewhere back when.

Our big outdoor dog was a black, lovable, full-blooded Labrador named "Rodie", short for "Sage Creek's Rodeo", his AKC registration.

Rodie was rather laid back. Whether he was on the deck of the chalet lolling in the afternoon sun, or in his kennel, deer, elk or moose wandering about were none of his concern. Even the occasional bear, appearing on the slope above the lodge, elicited barely a growl.

Rabbits and squirrels, however, were not to be tolerated, as they were totally undisciplined . . . racing thru the gardens and wild

roses, climbing trees, wiggling their noses, flashing their tails . . . and worst of all, eating Nancy's herbs and trying to get at the birdseed.

Wootsee, on the other hand, was in charge of everything and everybody—THE BOSS! When he decided Rodie had enough of a nap, he'd badger him until the two were covering the whole yard in circles and double-backs . . . Rodie in long lazy strides, Wootsee, in a blur of legs whirling several inches off the ground . . . covering the same distance.

Wootsee slept under our bed. When he decided we'd had enough sleep, (almost always before the sun was up) he'd leap onto the bed and start washing our faces. We may just as well have had a bugler sounding reveille . . . the night was over.

One spring morning, following the usual wakeup procedure, I grabbed my robe, stepped into my slippers, descended the narrow staircase from the loft, and opened the door for Wootsee to go into the wilderness for his morning's jaunt. He took off like a shot for the bird-feeder, where a squirrel was gleaning the seed husks at the base, looking for little tidbits. In a flash, the squirrel was up a nearby tree scolding Wootsee for interrupting his search.

Needing more wood for the stove, I turned in the other direction to pick up an arm load from the stack at the side of the chalet. I had just bent over when Nancy opened the window above me and said, quietly but with great urgency in her voice, "Brannon! Behind you!" I whirled around to find myself face to face with a huge bull moose. He was between me and the kennel, and had obviously been grazing there while Rodie slept.   At the sound of Nancy's voice, Rodie woke up, and seeing me on the other side of a moose, decided the situation called for a guard dog!   He let go everything he had with a machine gun staccato bark!

Wootsee rounded the corner of the chalet, responding to Rodie's bark, to take charge. All four feet a blur, and seeming suspended several inches in the air, he charged the moose.

A ball of black fur, coming at him like a speeding miniature locomotive . . . all the while sounding a high pitched bark, an echo of the monster dog at his back, about to close jaws on his hamstring . . . was too much. The moose leaped into the air and whirled for the creek, dirt flying in every direction as he dug every hoof deep for traction. Nearly a thousand pounds of huge bull moose thundering toward the creek with ten pounds of smartaleck puppy in hot pursuit.

As if someone threw a switch, the moose slammed on the brakes and slid to a stop at the edge of the creek. He whirled around and lowered his massive rack to face his adversary.

Without missing a stride, all four feet still a blur, Wootsee performed a perfect 180 degree about-face and made a beeline for me, executing a grand leap into my arms just as the moose dug in for the charge.

A long moment of silence. Rodie, his tail wagging like crazy, looked at me then at the moose and back to me again. Wootsee proceeded to lick my chin as a belated thank you. The moose seemed frozen in indecision.

Mr. Moose gave a shrug and shake, lowered his head and commenced to graze. Rodie lay down quietly in his kennel to watch sleepy-eyed.

INVOLTINI DI MANZO
Sausage and Spinach Stuffed Beef Steak

A hearty main dish that freezes well...nice to have on hand when company comes!

1 large round steak, about ½" thick
1 large Carrot, finely shredded
1 10-ounce package frozen Chopped Spinach
2 tablespoons Olive Oil
1 cup Beef Broth
1 cup Dry Red Wine
1 28-ounce can Italian Style Pear Tomatoes, chopped
1 recipe POLPETTE DI SALSICCIA

Place the round steak on a counter top, and cover it with a sheet of plastic wrap. Pound the steak with a flat mallet to tenderize it. Remove the plastic wrap, and spread the Italian Sausage mixture over the steak. Top that with the shredded carrot. Defrost the chopped spinach by placing it in a collander and putting it under hot, running water. Squeeze as much of the water out of the spinach as you can, and distribute the spinach evenly over the steak. Starting with the short side, roll up the steak, "jelly-roll" style, and tie it up with kitchen twine. Brown the steak on all sides in a roasting pan on the stove over medium-high heat. Then add the beef broth, the red wine and the tomatoes (juice and all). Cover the pan and place it in a preheated 375 degree oven for 1½ to 2 hours, or until is feels tender when pierced with a fork.

TO SERVE: Slice the involtini into rounds approximately ¾ inch thick. Place the slices on a warm platter and top with some of the sauce. If you like, serve a little pasta along side!

SPECIAL TIP: This is a fabulous dish to prepare in a "crock-pot"! Just brown the stuffed steak in a skillet first...add the remaining ingredients...and then transfer it to the "crock-pot" and let it go for several hours!

STORAGE INFORMATION: Once cooked, the stuffed steak will keep in the refrigerator for 1 week...in the freezer for up to 90 days.

PREPARATION TIME: 3 hours

YIELD: Serves 4 to 6

RAVIOLI DI BERGAMO
Meat-filled Ravioli in the style of Bergamo

A cable railway links modern Bergamo (in Lombardy) with its historic upper town, rich with medevial buildings, sculptures and paintings. We thought you might enjoy the delicate flavors of this simple dish, native to that town.

1 recipe BASIC EGG PASTA
1 clove Garlic, minced
2 tablespoons fresh Parsley, chopped
4 tablespoons Butter
¾ pound Lean Ground Beef
⅓ cup Bread Crumbs
¼ cup grated Parmesan Cheese
2 large Eggs, beaten
Salt and Pepper to taste
Dash of Nutmeg
½ cup (1 stick) Butter
Grated Parmesan Cheese to garnish

Let the pasta dough rest at room temperature. Melt the butter in a medium skillet and gently saute the garlic and parsley for 1 to 2 minutes. Add the beef, and continue sauteing until the me steel blade. Process the mixture on high for 30 seconds, or until the meat is finely chopped. Roll out the pasta (one sheet at a time) VERY THIN. Place the sheet of pasta on a clean, dry countertop, and brush it lightly with a pastry brush dipped in water. (This will help the raviolis to seal better, so they won't come apart during cooking!) If you are using a pasta machine that rolls a sheet of pasta about 5 inches wide, place rounded tea-spoons of the filling along one side in a single row, about 1½ inches apart. Fold the sheet of pasta in half, lengthwise, with the filling inside. Using a knife or fluted pastry cutter (or a ravioli cutter, if you have one!), cut the ravioli into squares. Place them on a clean, dry towel to lightly air dry. When all the raviolis are made, begin to cook them in boiling water, a few at a time. (Fresh raviolis need only a couple of minutes to cook...so be careful not to over cook them.) Meanwhile, in a small skillet, melt the butter...and even brown it a little, if you like. (If you let the butter brown slightly and then pour it over the ravioli, that is a sauce called BURRO VERSATO!) Top with a little grated Parmesan Cheese and serve hot.

VARIATION: If you prefer, top the raviolis with SALSA DI POMODORO.

STORAGE INFORMATION: The ravioli can be made up ahead, and either cov-ered with plastic wrap and refrigerated for several hours in advance, or frozen and then gathered up and stored in a plastic bag amd stored for up to 3 months.

PREPARATION TIME: 1 hour

YIELD: 6 servings

GAROFOLATO DI MANZO
Braised Beef with Cloves

A savory dish that has it's origin in Latium, you'll enjoy making GAROFOLATO DI MANZO for family, as well as friends. A great dish for the working person...you can simmer it in your slow cooker all day! The name comes from the Italian word...garofanare...to season with cloves! Serve it with a side dish of buttered pasta or rice.

Fresh Beef Brisket (approximately 2 pounds)
2 tablespoons Olive Oil
1 cup Dry Red Wine
1 28-ounce can Italian Style Pear Tomatoes, Chopped
2 cups Beef Broth
2 cloves Garlic, minced
6 to 10 Whole Cloves
Salt and Freshly Ground Black Pepper to taste

In a large Dutch oven, heat the olive oil over medium-high heat and brown the brisket well on both sides. Take the pan from the stove, and add the remaining ingredients. If you have a slow-cooker, put the contents of the pan into the it, and let it simmer all day. If not, cover the Dutch oven, and place it in a 300 degree oven and slow-roast for several hours, or until it feels tender when pierced with a fork. The length of time will vary, depending on the thickness and quality of the cut of meat.

STORAGE INFORMATION: Once cooked, this dish will keep in the refrigerator for several days, or in the freezer for up to 60 days. It re-heats VERY well.

PREPARATION TIME: 30 minutes, plus time to simmer

YIELD: 4 to 6 servings

BISTECCA ALLA FIORENTINA
Steak Florentine

A classic dish from Tuscany, the people of Florence proudly serve to their finest guests. It is traditionally made using what we would call a Porterhouse Steak. When we served it on the feast, we felt that most of our guests could not consume that much meat along with the rest of their feast. So, we chose Beef Tenderloin, instead. With today's lighter appetites, we still think that this is a better choice! We accompanied this dish with FUNGHI TRIFOLATI...wonderful sauteed wild and domestic mushrooms.

2 pounds Prime Beef Tenderloin (about 8 ounces per person)
¼ cup Extra Virgin Olive Oil (a good fruity one!)
Salt and freshly ground Black Pepper
Lemon Wedges

Florentine Steak must NEVER be over cooked! If you can, cook it outside on a very hot grill. (If not outside, then the oven broiler will have to do!) Cut the beef into 4 steaks about 1 inch thick, depending on the diameter of the tenderloin. Place them on the grill, about 3 inches from the coals (or gas flame). Sear them well on the first side, before turning. Then sear the second side. Florentines want their steak as rare as they can get it, while still having the center hot. Cook them the way you and your guests like them...but please...not well done! When they're ready, remove them to a heated platter. Add salt and pepper and drizzle them with the olive oil. Serve with the lemon wedges, instructing your guests to squeeze the lemon over the top, before eating.

STORAGE INFORMATION: Make and serve immediately.

PREPARATION TIME: 20 minutes

YIELD: 4 servings

MAIALE ARROSTO AFFETTATO
Roast Pork Tenderloin

Slow-roasted for tenderness, this method of preparation also provides additional moisture to allow for the meat to be roasted well done, and yet not be dry.

2 Pork Tenderloins
2 teaspoons Juniper Berries
1 teaspoon minced Garlic
1 tablespoon Olive Oil
Coarse Ground Black Pepper

With a mortar and pestle, crush the juniper berries, then add the garlic and olive oil...stir to combine. Place the tenderloins in a shallow pan. Top with the juniper berry mixture, spreading it over the surface of the tenderloins. Add a generous grinding of black pepper. Insert a meat thermometer into the thickest part of one of the tenderloins at a long, low angle so as to get the most accurate reading. Place the pan in a preheated 350 degree oven for approximately 1 hour, or until internal temperature has reached 175 to 180 degrees. Serve hot, as an entree, with a side dish such as Fettucine Alfredo (see SALSA ALFREDO)...or at room temperature as an appetizer with a tangy mustard sauce, called SALSA DI SENAPE, for dipping.

STORAGE INFORMATION: This dish can be made up to 3 days ahead, wrapped in plastic wrap (not foil!) and stored in the refrigerator, or frozen for up to 3 months! To serve, just bring to room temperature (or heat), and serve.

PREPARATION TIME: A little more than 1 hour.

YIELD: 4 entree-size servings...6 to 8 appetizer-size servings

POLPETTE DI SALSICCIA
Sausage Meatballs

This versatile recipe is the nucleus for a variety of main dishes and appetizers from all over Italy! Having the mixture on hand in the freezer makes a lot of sense! You can serve the meatballs on a bed of pasta, topped with your favorite red sauce...as an appetizer with red sauce, sweet and sour sauce, or mustard sauce for dipping...or use this same mixture in INVOLTINI DI MANZO, or FUNGHI RIPIENI.

1 to 1½ pounds Italian Sausage (sweet or hot, your preference)
2 large Eggs, lightly beaten
¼ teaspoon Garlic Powder
1 teaspoon Oregano
1 tablespoon Minced Onion
1 tablespoon chopped fresh Parsley Bread Crumbs

Combine the first six ingredients in the work bowl of a food processor fitted with a steel blade. Process for 30 seconds, scraping the sides of the work bowl at least once during that time. Place the meat in a medium size bowl, and add enough bread crumbs to make the mixture hold together. Shape into meatballs. Place them into a shallow baking tray and put them into a preheated 400 degree oven for about 25 to 35 minutes, or until them brown lightly. Shake the tray from time to time, to turn the meatballs and cook them evenly. The cooking time will vary, depending on the size of the meatballs.

SPECIAL TIPS: Shaping the meatballs is a lot easier if you moisten your hands first! The water will keep the meat mixture from sticking to your hands, and allow you to make the shapes for uniform. You'll need to moisten your hand several times during the shaping process.

STORAGE INFORMATION: Cooked meatballs can be stored in the refrigerator for up to 4 days...in the freezer for up to 90 days.

PREPARATION TIME: 40 minutes

YIELD: 24 to 30 medium size meatballs

LASAGNE ALLA CALABRESE
Meatball Lasagne in the style of Calabria

This lasagne has nothing to do with the "American-ized" versions you get here. The pasta is delicate...it has meatballs inside...it contains three varieties of cheese...artichokes...and the red sauce is on the INSIDE, not on the outside! Your guests will truly be amazed!

1 recipe BASIC EGG PASTA (at room temperature)
1 recipe POLPETTE DI SALSICCIA (Sausage Meatballs), cooked
1 cup SALSA DI POMODORO (Tomato Sauce), warm
1 cup BALSAMELLA (Bechamel Sauce), warm
1 14-ounce can Artichoke Hearts
(drained and sauteed in 2 tablespoons Butter)
1 15-ounce tub Ricotta Cheese
6 ounces Mozzarella Cheese, sliced
1 cup grated Parmesan Cheese

Have all the ingredients gathered before you begin to assemble the lasagne. Roll the pasta a thin as you can. If you are doing it by hand, roll it into rounds 9" in diameter. (You will need 10 rounds to complete the lasagne.) If you are using a pasta machine that yields a 5 to 6 inch wide strip, cut the pasta into semi-circles, using the bottom of a springform pan. (In that case, you will need 20 half-circles. You can also use the springform pan bottom to make the hand-rolled circle more even. As you roll and cut the pasta, lay the finished circles (or semi-circles) onto clean, dry towels. When you have them all cut, bring a large pot of water to a boil over medium-high heat. Meanwhile, fill a large mixing bowl with ice cold water. Cook the pasta rounds, one or two at a time, for about 90 seconds, or until al dente. As soon as they are done, plunge them into the bowl of cold water to stop the cooking process. Leave them in the water until you are ready to assemble the lasagne. Put a spoonful of the tomato sauce into the bottom of a 9 inch springform pan...distributing it evenly. On top of that, place a round of pasta (or two halves). Then cover the pasta with a single layer of the mozzarella...then another layer of pasta. Then distribute the artichoke hearts evenly for the next layer. Top with another layer of pasta. Arrange the meatballs evenly over that layer, and top with tomato sauce. Spread the sauce evenly over the meatballs, using the back of the spoon to fill the crevices. Top with a layer of pasta. Drain any excess water from the ricotta cheese, and break the cheese into pieces over the last layer. Using a spatula, smooth the ricotta to an even layer about ¼ inch thick. Top with pasta. Using your hands, press evenly over the surface of the last layer to "settle" the lasagne. Top with warm bechamel. Distribute evenly. Finally, add the grated Parmesan and, using your finger-tips, smooth it out to within ½ inch of the edge of the pan. Bake in a preheated 375 degree oven for about 1 hour, or until the top is a nice golden brown. Cut into wedges and serve hot.

SPECIAL TIP: If you make the lasagne a day or so ahead and refrigerate it, the wedges you cut while it's cold, will be neater and more attractive. Just place them in individual baking dishes and warm in a 400 degree oven for 15 minutes before serving.

STORAGE INFORMATION: Will keep wrapped in plastic wrap in the refrigerator for 4 or 5 days...or in the freezer for up to 2 months.

PREPARATION TIME: 2 hours

YIELD: 12 servings

PETTI DI TACCHINO RIPIENI
Veal Stuffed Breast of Turkey

YIELD: 6 servings

Delightful all year round, we found this recipe particularly nice in the spring and summer, when the vegetables are at their best and appetites are light and lively!

1 Whole Turkey Breast (NOT a rolled turkey roast!)
1 pound Ground Veal
2 large Eggs
2 tablespoons Dry Bread Crumbs
½ teaspoon Oregano
¼ teaspoon Garlic Powder
1 small Onion, minced
½ teaspoon Salt
A few grindings of Black Pepper
1 8-ounce package frozen Asparagus Spears
(or an equal amount of FRESH Asparagus, if available, blanched)
4 tablespoons melted Butter
1 recipe SALSA DI POMODORI FRESCHI

Bone the turkey breast, and remove the skin, leaving the breast whole. Lay it flat on the countertop, and cover it with plastic wrap. Pound it lightly with a wooden malet to flatten and tenderize it. Next, make the filling. Combine all the remaining ingredients (except the asparagus spears and the melted butter) in a large bowl. Mix well. (I use my hands for this procedure. I don't believe that man has ever invented two more efficient tools than our hands!) Spread the meat mixture evenly over the inside of the turkey breast. Then, top with the asparagus spears, distributing them evenly over the surface. Roll the whole breast up, jelly roll style, and tie it up with kitchen twine. Brush the surface with the melted butter, reserving any extra for a second basting later. Place the stuffed breast in a covered roasting pan (or cover your pan with foil) and place it in a 325 degree oven for about 1½ to 2 hours, or until a meat thermometer indicates an internal temperature of 180 to 185 degrees. Meanwhile, make the SALSA DI POMODORI FRESCHI. Take the finished roast from the oven and let it "rest" for 5 to 10 minutes before slicing. Then slice and top with the SALSA DI POMODORI FRESCHI. Serve hot...perhaps with a little pasta on the side, topped with a spoonful of the sauce!

SPECIAL TIP: To make all rolled roasts easier, ask your butcher if he will sell you a foot or so of an item they call "Jet Net"...an elastic netting that holds your stuffed roast firmly in place during cooking. Many butchers use it for boned and rolled roasts they sell in their store. If you tell him why you need it, I'm sure he'll happily oblige.

STORAGE INFORMATION: Keeps well, roast and unsliced in the refrigerator for 3 or 4 days, or in the freezer for up to 3 months. Just take it out, put it in a foil covered pan and heat thru...slice and serve.

PREPARATION TIME: 3 hours (including baking time).

CROCCHETTE Di POLLO
Chicken Croquettes

Served as an entree topped with SALSA ALFREDO...or without the sauce as an appetizer...your guests will love these moist and tender morsels!

2 pounds boneless, skinless Chicken Thighs
1 cup BALSAMELLA
2 tablespoons dried Parsley Flakes
½ cup finely chopped Prosciutto
½ cup grated Parmesan Cheese
Enough Bread Crumbs to coat the croquettes
Vegetable Oil for deep frying

Put the chicken thighs in a large stock pot and cover with water. Put on the stove top on medium heat and simmer for at least 1 hour, or until tender. Set aside and allow to cool. Take the chicken thighs from the broth and remove and discard the skin and bones...reserving the meat for the croquettes. (Save the broth for a nice soup!) In a food processor fitted with a steel blade, combine the remaining ingredients, all but the bread crumbs and the vegetable oil. Shape into small cone shapes, and roll in the bread crumbs. Place the croquettes onto a tray lined with wax paper. At this point, they can be covered with plastic wrap until you are ready to deep fry them. In a deep fryer, or a large sauce pan, heat the oil to about 375 degrees. Deep fry a few at a time and keep hot in a 250 degree oven until ready to serve.

SERVING SUGGESTION: Serve topped with SALSA ALFREDO as a main entree... or without sauce as an exciting appetizer!

SPECIAL TIP: Allow the croquettes to come to room temperature before deep frying. In that way, the centers will be as hot as the outsides!

STORAGE INFORMATION: Store them (covered) in the refrigerator for up to four hours before deep frying. Or, freeze them on a baking tray...then gather them up and put them in a plastic container. Frozen, they'll keep for up to 3 months. In either case, bring them to room temperature before deep frying.

PREPARATION TIME: 2 hours

YIELD: 4 servings

POLLO CON FUNGHI
Chicken with Mushrooms

An easy, elegant and delightful way to serve everyone's favorite...CHICKEN!

4 pounds boneless, skinless Chicken Breasts
½ cup Flour
½ teaspoon EACH Salt and Pepper
3 tablespoons EACH Butter and Olive Oil
1 pound fresh Mushrooms, sliced
1½ cups Chicken Broth
1 tablespoon Lemon Juice
½ cup White Wine
Dash of Nutmeg
1 cup Heavy Whipping Cream
1 to 2 tablespoons chopped fresh Parsley
Salt and Pepper to taste
Enough Gold Medal Wondra to thicken sauce as desired

Rinse the chicken pieces under cold, running water, and dredge them in a mixture of the flour, salt and pepper. In a large skillet, melt the butter and olive oil over medium heat, and saute the chicken pieces until golden brown. Reduce the heat, and continue to simmer for 30 to 40 minutes, turning occasionally. Remove the chicken from the skillet...place it on a platter and keep it warm in a 250 degree oven while you make the sauce. To the same skillet, add the mushrooms (and a little extra butter, if needed) and saute for 5 minutes. Then add the chicken broth, lemon juice and white wine...boiling vigorously for 3 to 4 minutes. (Be sure to scrape any bits of the browned chicken and mushrooms from the sides and bottom of the pan.) Lower the heat, and stir in the whipping cream, and the nutmeg. Thicken the sauce with a sprinkle or two of Gold Medal Wondra. Simmer...and add salt and pepper to taste. Pour the sauce over the chicken, and top with chopped fresh parsley.

SPECIAL TIP: You can make this dish up to a day or two ahead. Just refrigerate the chicken and the sauce in seperate containers. Heat the sauce in a skillet...the chicken in the oven. Combine just before serving!

STORAGE INFORMATION: Sauce and chicken can be stored seperately in the refrigerator for up to 2 days.

PREPARATION TIME: 1 hour

YIELD: 4 Servings

POLLO AL PROSCIUTTO
Chicken with Parma Ham

An easy, nutritious and TASTY main course!

1½ to 2 pounds boneless, skinless Chicken Thighs
1 stick Butter
1 teaspoon dried Basil (or 2 teaspoons of FRESH)
4 to 6 ounces Prosciutto, sliced wafer thin
1 tablespoon dried Parsley Flakes (or 2 tablespoons of FRESH)

Melt the butter in a small skillet, and add the Basil and Parsley. Rinse the chicken under cold, running water. Pat dry. Dip the chicken into the melted butter, and wrap each one in a slice of the Prosciutto. Place them in a buttered baking dish, and drizzle any remaining butter/herb mixture over the top. Place them in a preheated 375 degree oven COVERED, for 45 minutes, or until tender.

STORAGE INFORMATION: These can be made up ahead and frozen, UNCOOKED for up to 30 days.

PREPARATION TIME: 1 hour

YIELD: 4 servings

COZZE CON VINO
Fresh Mussels with Wine Sauce

In the Rocky Mountains, fresh mussels are very hard to come by. They've always been a personal favorite of mine, and so I used the feast as an excuse to have them on hand regularly!

2 tablespoons Extra Virgin Olive Oil
1 teaspoon minced fresh Garlic
½ cup Dry White Wine
(a Frascati or Pinot Grigio would be delightful!)
1 tablespoon fresh Basil, chopped
(or half that much if you use dried Basil)
A sprinkling of dried Red Pepper Flakes (optional)
1 tablespoon fresh Parsley, chopped
Salt and freshly ground pepper to taste
40 fresh Mussels, scrubbed and debearded
Fresh Lemon Wedges

Heat the oil in a large skillet (one with a lid) and saute the garlic over medium-high heat for 1 minute. Add the wine, the herbs, and then the mussels. Cover and steam the mussels for 6 to 8 minutes, or until all the shells are open. Taste the sauce and add salt and pepper to your own personal taste. Put the mussels in a pre-warmed deep platter (or shallow bowl) and pour the sauce over the top. Serve hot, garnished with fresh lemon wedges.

SERVING SUGGESTION: When we had this dish on the feast, we served it atop a bed of Angel Hair Linguini...and it was stupendous!

SPECIAL TIPS: When mussels are fresh (and alive), the shells are closed. When cleaning the mussels, discard any that are open. Scrub them well with a vegetable brush and rinse several times in cold water. Allow them to sit in the final rinse water for 20 to 30 minutes. This will cleanse them of any sandy residue. Then, with a knife, trim off the "beards" before cooking.

STORAGE INFORMATION: The mussels will keep for 2 or 3 days in the refrigerator covered with a wet towel. Do not seal them in a plastic container, as you will kill the mussels before you are ready to cook them.

PREPARATION TIME: 30 minutes

YIELD: 4 servings

ROTOLO DI PESCE
Crab Stuffed Sole Filets

In an era when many people are trying to balance their diets with less red meats, ROTOLO DI PESCE answers that need in a delicious way!

8 small Filets of Sole
1 6-ounce can Snow Crab meat
1 large Egg, lightly beaten
Grated Peel of 1 Lemon
1 to 2 teaspoons chopped, fresh Parsley
Enough Bread Crumbs to bind the mixture
Salt and freshly ground Black Pepper
2 to 3 tablespoons Butter

Rinse the sole filets under cold, running water. Pat them dry with paper towels and set them aside, while you make the filling. Drain the crab meat and place it in a small bowl with the egg, lemon peel and chopped parsley. Add enough dry bread crumbs to make the mixture fairly firm. Add salt and pepper to taste. Distribute the mixture evenly over the filets, and roll them up like pinwheels. Place them, flat side down, in a buttered baking dish, and dot each one with butter. Bake them in a preheated 375 degree oven for 25 to 30 minutes, or until the flesh of the fish is firm and white, and the butter is bubbly. Serve hot.

VARIATION: If you like, top the pinwheels with a spoonful of BALSAMELLA.

STORAGE INFORMATION: Make these up ahead, and store them, uncooked, in the refrigerator for several hours before baking, or in the freezer for up to 30 days.

PREPARATION TIME: 1 hour

YIELD: 4 servings

PESCE AL CARTOCCIO
Fish Baked in Parchment

A lovely way to prepare and present fish. This same recipe works equally well for crab or shrimp!

8 small or 4 larger Filets of Sole (or other fish of your choice)
1 small Onion, thinly sliced
1 large Carrot, cut into thin julienne strips
4 slices of fresh Lemon, approximately ¼" thick
4 large, fresh Basil Leaves (or a sprinkling of dried Basil)
4 tablespoons Butter, melted
Salt to taste
Baking Parchment

Cut the baking parchment into 4 squares approximately 10" X 10". Lay them flat on the countertop, and place a fish filet on top of each. Top that with some onion, carrot and a basil leaf on each. Drizzle 1 tablespoon of butter over each packet, and sprinkle with a tiny bit of salt. Place a lemon slice on the very top, and fold the parchment over all. Try to get the packet sealed as tightly as you can...tucking the ends underneath. Place the packets on a baking sheet and bake them in a preheated 400 degree oven for 20 to 30 minutes, depending on the thickness of the filets.

STORAGE INFORMATION: This dish can be made assembled up to 4 hours ahead, and baked and served when your guests arrive!

PREPARATION TIME: 45 minutes

YIELD: 4 servings

CAPESANTE ALLA FIORENTINA
Scallops Florentine Style

A dish so simple, yet so elegant, you'll want to reserve it for very special occasions! Whether you use the tiny "Bay" scallops, or the larger "Sea" scallops, this is a dish destined for special occasions!

2 tablespoons Butter
1 cup Heavy Whipping Cream
Sprinkle ground White Pepper
1 teaspoon Parsley Flakes
Dash Garlic Powder
Salt to taste
Gold Medal Wondra to thicken
1 10-ounce package frozen Chopped Spinach
1 tablespoon Butter
Salt and Pepper to taste
1 to 1½ pounds Scallops
1 cup Dry White Wine
2 tablespoons chopped fresh Parsley

For the Sauce: Melt 2 tablespoons butter in a medium skillet. Then add the cream, pepper and parsley flakes. Bring the sauce to a gentle boil over medium heat, and season with a little garlic powder...salt to taste. Just a hint of the garlic! Don't overwhelm the flavor of the sauce! Thicken with a sprinkling of the Gold Medal Wondra...whisking to incorporate it into the sauce. Keep the sauce warm on a back burner, and cook the package of chopped spinach according to package directions. When it is cooked, drain it well, and add the tablespoon of butter. Toss well, and season with salt and pepper to taste. Again, keep it warm on a back burner. Finally, cook the scallops by dropping them into a small saucepan of simmering white wine. Bring them back up to a simmer and TURN THEM OFF...leaving them in place on the burner for a few minutes. (See "Special Tips") Place generous servings of the buttered spinach into individual baking dishes, topping it with the scallops, and then some of the sauce. Garnish with a sprinkling of fresh chopped parsley. VARIATION: Substitute Baby Shrimp or Clams for the Scallops.

SPECIAL TIP: Be sure not to boil the scallops. Just bring the wine to a simmer...drop in the scallops...bring them back up to a simmer...and turn them off (leaving them on the burner for a few minutes). The residual heat from the wine, hot pan, and burner, will be more than sufficient to cook the scallops. When they're firm...they're done!

STORAGE INFORMATION: The sauce can be made a day or so ahead...just store it in the refrigerator in a covered, plastic container.

PREPARATION TIME: 30 minutes

YIELD: 4 servings

RISOTTO CON GAMBERETTI
Risotto with Baby Shrimp

A wonderfully flavorful main dish that you prepare in a skillet!

3 tablespoons Olive Oil
½ cup (1 stick) Butter
1 small Onion, minced
1 teaspoon chopped Fresh Garlic
1 cup Clam Juice
4 cups Chicken Broth
2 cups imported Italian Arborio Rice
½ cup Dry White Wine
1 28-ounce can Whole Peeled Italian-style Pear Tomatoes
(drained, most seeds removed, chopped)
4 tablespoons chopped fresh Parsley (or 2 tablespoons of dried Parsley Flakes)
1 pound frozen, pre-cooked Baby Shrimp, defrosted and rinsed
(about 3 cups when still frozen)
Salt and freshly ground Black Pepper to taste

In a large skillet, melt the butter and olive oil over medium heat. Add the onions and garlic and saute until the onions are limp. Meanwhile, in a sauce pan, heat the broth and clam juice to a near boil. Reduce the heat to low. To the onions, add the uncooked rice and stir well, until the rice is glazed and slightly shiny. Add a ladle full of the broth, and stir well. Continue adding the broth, ONE LADLE AT A TIME, allowing each ladle full to be absorbed before adding the next. After a few minutes, add the wine. Continue to stir well after each addition...until the rice is done. You may not use all of the broth...or may require the addition of a little water at the end, depending on the accuracy of your measurements. Just before the rice is done, add the remaining ingredients and stir well. Continue cooking until most of the liquid is absorbed. Season with salt and pepper to taste. Serve hot.

SPECIAL TIP: How to tell when the rice is done: The rice should be firm, but not chalky...and the grains must cling together in a creamy base. When eaten, each grain of rice should have a definite "bite" to the center.

STORAGE INFORMATION: This dish can be made several hours ahead. Prepare the rice up to the point where you add the tomatoes, parsley and shrimp. Spread it out on a baking sheet to cool and stop the cooking process. About 10 minutes before serving time, heat the rice in a skillet and finish as usual.

PREPARATION TIME: 40 minutes

YIELD: 4 to 6 servings

AGNOLOTTI DI GRANCHI
Crescent Shaped Crab Meat Ravioli

While a totally original recipe we devised for the Fall Feast of 1988, it's origins are from the area around the Gulf of Genoa, in the Thyrhenian Sea. Light and delicate, we top them with BURRO VERSATO (browned butter sauce), a simple grating of Parmigiano-Reggiano, and a spiral of fresh lemon.

1 pound of Crab Meat (Dungeoness or Snow Crab...canned or frozen)
2 Egg Yolks
2 cloves Garlic, minced
1 tablespoon dried Parsley (or 2 tablespoons of fresh)
1 bunch Green Onions, chopped (tops only)
¼ cup freshly grated Parmesan Cheese
Approximately ½ cup Dry Bread Crumbs
Salt and Pepper to taste
1 recipe BASIC EGG PASTA (or Spinach Pasta, if you prefer)
1 Whole Egg, beaten
6 to 8 tablespoons Butter
2 tablespoons fresh Lemon Juice
1 whole, fresh Lemon

Have the pasta dough made up ahead and resting at room temperature for at least 30 minutes before assembly. Drain the crab meat, and squeeze as much of the water out as you can. Combine all the ingredients (except the pasta dough and the whole egg) in the work bowl of a food processor fitted with a steel blade. Process for several seconds, or until the mixture is chopped fine, and well blended. Check the consistancy, and add more bread crumbs if needed, so that the mixture holds its shape well when formed into a lump. Taste the filling, and add Salt and Pepper to suit your own taste. Roll out the pasta dough as thin as you can manage (we use the thinnest setting on our roller-type machine), and cut it into 1½ to 2 inch rounds. Holding the pasta circle in your hand, brush the edges lightly with beaten egg. Place a scant ½ teaspoon of the crab mixture on one half of the circle and fold it over, sealing the edges with your fingers. Place the agnolotti on the countertop, and crimp the edges with the tines of a fork. As you get them assembled, lay the agnolotti onto a clean, dry terry cloth towel to lightly air dry. Place a large sauce pan of water over high heat and bring it to a boil. While you're waiting for the water to boil, make the sauce, called BURRO VERSATO...or "browned butter". In a small skillet, melt the butter until it begins to brown slightly. Set it aside and keep it warm while you cook the agnolotti. When the agnolotti are done (don't over cook!), pour them into a collander to quickly drain...then back into the pot in which you cooked them. Then, pour the BURRO VERSATO over the top, followed by the fresh Lemon Juice. Slice the Lemon into ⅛ inch slices and then cut half way into the center and twist them into a "spiral". Place the agnolotti on a warm serving platter and garnish with the lemon spirals. Serve hot.

SPECIAL TIP: These agnolotti are easiest to serve without overcooking, if you freeze them first! If you choose to do that, as you assemble them, place them on a baking tray lined with a double layer of wax paper. Fill the tray, cover them with plastic wrap and freeze! Then gather them up and put them in a plastic container. Then just drop them into boiling water (frozen) to cook.

STORAGE INFORMATION: Store (covered) in the refrigerator for several hours before serving...or in the freezer for up to 60 days.

PREPARATION TIME: 1 to ½ hours

YIELD: About 4 dozen ravioli

SALTIMBOCCA ALLA SORRENTINA
Veal Topped with Prosciutto and Fresh Tomato Sauce

From Sorrento, in the south of Italy, not far from Naples, we bring you this exciting dish. Tender slices of veal...topped with Prosciutto, Mozzarella, Fresh Tomato Sauce and Parmesan Cheese. A winner!

1 to 1½ pounds Veal Sirloin, sliced very thin
4 tablespoons Butter
4 ounces Prosciutto, sliced wafer thin
6 ounces Mozzarella Cheese, thinly sliced
1 recipe SALSA DI POMODORI FRESCHI
3 to 4 ounces grated Parmesan Cheese
(preferably Parmigiano-Reggiano)

Place the slices of veal on a cutting board. Cover them with plastic wrap, and pound them lightly with a wooden mallet, until very thin. In a large skillet, saute the veal slices (a few at a time) in the butter over medium heat, until tender and golden brown...about 15 minutes. Remove them from the skillet, and place them in a flat, oven-proof baking dish. When they are all cooked, top each piece of veal with a slice of prosciutto...then a slice of mozzarella...then a spoonful of the SALSA DI POMODORI FRESCHI and then top it all off with a generous sprinkling of Parmesan. Bake in a preheated 400 degree oven for 15 to 20 minutes, or until the cheeses are melted and lightly golden brown.

STORAGE INFORMATION: This dish can be made up several hours ahead, covered with plastic wrap, and stored in the refrigerator. Just bake and enjoy.

PREPARATION TIME: 45 minutes

YIELD: 4 servings

VITELLO FARCITO
Stuffed Veal Rolls

A grand Veal dish...fit for kings...and queens!

1½ to 2 pounds thinly sliced Veal Sirloin Steak
¼ to ½ pound Prosciutto, thinly sliced
1 10-ounce package frozen Chopped Spinach
¼ cup Onion, minced
6 tablespoons Butter
1¼ cups (about 10 ounces) Ricotta Cheese
1 Egg, lightly beaten
Enough Bread Crumbs to bind
Salt and Pepper to taste
3 tablespoons Olive Oil
1 cup Chicken Broth
1 cup Vermouth
2 Bay Leaves

Place the steak on a clean, dry countertop and cover it with a sheet of plastic wrap. Pound the steak lightly with a flat, wooden mallet to tenderize it. Cut it into individual serving pieces, and set them aside. Defrost the spinach, by placing it in a colander under hot, running water. Squeeze as much of the water from the spianch as you can, and set it aside. Saute the onion in the butter until transparent. Then add the spinach and continue sauteing for 5 minutes. Remove the mixture from the heat, and place it in a medium size bowl. Add the ricotta, egg and enough bread crumbs to lightly bind the mixture together. Add salt and pepper to taste. Lay the pieces of veal out on the countertop, and cover them each with a thin slice of the prosciutto. Distribute the spinach and ricotta filling evenly over the tops, and roll them up "jelly roll" style...securing them with a toothpick. In an large skillet, heat the olive oil, and saute the bay leaves for 1 minute. Then, add the veal rolls, and brown them over medium-high heat. When they are nicely browned on the outside, take them from the skillet and place them on a plate, while you make the sauce. To the skillet with the bay leaves, add the chicken broth and vermouth. Bring the sauce to a rapid boil, scraping any bits from the bottom and sides of the pan. Cook 4 or 5 minutes. Lower the heat to a simmer, and add the veal rolls...simmering for 30 to 40 minutes. Just before serving, adjust the seasoning, by adding salt and pepper to taste. Serve hot as an entree accompanied by POLENTA or buttered pasta.

STORAGE INFORMATION: This dish can be assembled up to several hours ahead and finished when your guest are due to arrive.

PREPARATION TIME: 1 to 1 ½ hours

YIELD: 4 servings

VITELLO AL MARSALA
Veal with Marsala Wine

An elegant dish that's quick and easy...perfect when the "boss" comes to dinner! Or your Mother-in-Law!

1 to 1½ pounds Veal Sirloin, sliced very thin
A scant cup Flour
2 tablespoons Extra Virgin Olive Oil
2 tablespoons Butter
½ cup Marsala Wine
Salt and freshly ground Pepper to taste

Place the veal on a cutting board. Cover it with plastic wrap and pound it with a wooden mallet until very thin. Coat the veal lightly with the flour, and set aside. In a large skillet, heat the olive oil and the butter over medium heat. Saute the veal slices until they are golden brown and tender...about 15 minutes. Towards the end of the cooking time, add the Marsala and raise the heat. When the alcohol has evaporated and the sauce has thickened, serve hot...perhaps, as we did, with angel hair linguini.

VARIATION: To make this dish more of a meal, try adding 6 to 8 fresh mushrooms (sliced) to the saute!

STORAGE INFORMATION: Pound the veal ahead of time and store it, covered, in the refrigerator until 20 minutes before serving time. Then just saute and finish the dish as usual.

PREPARATION TIME: 30 minutes

YIELD: 4 servings

CROSTATA RIPIENA DI BROCCOLI E RICOTTA
Broccoli and Ricotta Cheese Filled Pie

This recipe makes a wonderful vegetarian entree...or a great addition to an antipasto tray.

1 large bunch Broccoli, chopped
1 teaspoon fresh minced Garlic
¼ cup Olive Oil
½ cup chopped Onion
1 15-ounce tub Ricotta Cheese
3 large Eggs, beaten
Salt and Pepper to taste
1 recipe PASTA FROLLA II

Bring a large pot of water to a boil and add a sprinkling of salt to flavor the broccoli. Cook the broccoli for 5 to 7 minutes, or until it is 'tender crisp'. Drain well and set aside. Saute the onion and garlic in the olive oil until the onion is limp. Add the broccoli, stirring well. Season with salt and pepper to taste. Set aside to cool. Beat the eggs with a wire whisk and combine them with the ricotta. Add the broccoli/onion mixture and stir well. Meanwhile make the crust from my recipe for PASTA FROLLA II. Divide the dough into two parts...one slightly larger than the other. Using the larger "half", roll it out with a rolling pin to fit the bottom and up the sides of a 10 to 12 inch tart pan. Press it into place and then fill the shell with the broccoli mixture, distributing it evenly over the bottom. Coat the vertical sides of the bottom crust with a little water on a pastry brush. Roll out the top crust large enough to just cover the broccoli mixture. Put it into position, and then fold down the sides of the bottom crust and seal well. Prick the top with a fork or a sharp knife, and bake for about 1 hour in a pre-heated 375 degree oven, or until the crust is a deep, golden brown. Serve warm, or at room temperature.

SPECIAL TIP: This pie can also be made without a tart pan. Just place the bottom crust on a baking sheet...fill...place the top crust in place...fold the edges of the bottom crust over the top crust and crimp with a fork.

STORAGE INFORMATION: Make up the pie several hours ahead...cover with plastic wrap and refrigerate until about 1½ hours before serving time. Bake and serve as usual.

PREPARATION TIME: 1 hour 45 minutes (including baking time)

YIELD: 6 servings

FRITATTA

A sort of "omelet"...Italian style! Cut into pieces and served at room temperature, it makes a wonderful addition to an antipasto plate. It's also great as a luncheon or brunch entree...just cut into wedges and serve warm. You can vary this recipe to suit your mood...just add broccoli, mushrooms, artichokes, onions, zucchine...use your imagination!

6 large whole Eggs
Salt and Pepper to taste
2 tablespoons Butter
About 1 cup of your favorite vegetable, sliced or diced
1 tablespoon fresh Herbs, finely chopped
(pick your favorite...Basil...Oregano...Thyme)
(cut the amount in half if you use dried herbs)

With a wire whisk, lightly beat the eggs, and set them aside. In a medium skillet, melt the butter and saute the vegetables until "tender-crisp", adding salt and freshly ground pepper to taste. Remove them to a bowl, and let them cool. Then, incorporate them into the beaten eggs. Save the skillet, with the butter residue for baking the fritatta. Stir the egg and vegetable mixture well, and immediately our it into the skillet. Place the skillet on the stove top on medium heat. Once you see evidence that the fritatta is cooking around the edges, cover the skillet and reduce the heat to "low". From this point on...DO NOT STIR THE FRITATTA. Check the fritatta from time to time, but understand that it will take about 20 to 25 minutes for it to bake. Test it for doneness by gently shaking the skillet. When the center is firm, you're almost there! While you're waiting, preheat your oven to "broil", and move a rack to the top position. When the fritatta is firm, move the skillet to the broiler, and lightly brown the top. When it's done, take it out of the oven, and, using an egg turner, loosen it all the way around, and as far under the fritatta as you can reach. Again, shake the skillet gently, and make sure the fritatta is completely free on the bottom. Then, just slide it out of the skillet onto a cutting board.

SPECIAL TIP: Fritattas are FOOL-PROOF if you make them in a teflon-lined skillet!

STORAGE INFORMATION: Can be made several hours in advance, and stored at room temperature.

PREPARATION TIME: 30 minutes

YIELD: Serves 12 as an appetizer...6 as an entree

FOCACCIA FARCITA
Savory Stuffed Pizza

This is a wonderfully versatile recipe! You can stuff the "pizza" with tomatoes, cheese and onions…as we have done here, or make up your own combination! Try adding some thinly sliced Capocollo, Prosciutto or Salami…or sauteed Italian Sausage.

1 recipe FOCACCIA ALL'OLIO E SALE
2 large red, ripe Tomatoes, sliced very thin
1 large, sweet Onion, sliced very thin
8 ounces Mozzarella Cheese, shredded
Garlic Salt to taste
1 teaspoon dried Basil (or 2 teaspoons FRESH Basil, minced)
4 tablespoons Extra Virgin Olive Oil
1 Egg, beaten with 1 tablespoon water
Bread Crumbs

Make up the bread dough and cut it into two pieces…one slightly larger than the other. With a rolling pin, roll out the larger piece into a circle 14 inches in diameter. Oil a 12 inch pizza pan, using 1 tablespoon of the olive oil. Place the circle of dough on the pan. (You should have about 1 inch "extra" dough all around the edge.) Place the tomatoes in a single layer over the top of the dough. Top with a single layer of onions, and then cover with the cheese. Sprinkle with garlic salt and basil…then drizzle the remaining olive oil over the top. Roll out the top crust to a diameter of about 12 inches. With a sharp knife, make 1 to 2 inch slashes in the top crust in a decorative pattern. Gently pick up the top crust, and place it over the fillings. Using your fingers, fold the outer edge of the bottom crust over the outer edge of the top crust and flute…being sure to get a good seal all the way around. Brush the top and edges with the beaten egg and water mixture. Sprinkle bread crumbs evenly over the top. Bake in a preheated 400 degree oven for 25 to 30 minutes, or until deep golden brown. Serve hot.

STORAGE INFORMATION: Make the stuffed pizza up to an hour ahead. Cover with plastic wrap and store in the refrigerator until 30 minutes before serving time. Bake and serve as usual.

PREPARATION TIME: 1 hour

YIELD: 6 servings

ROTOLO DI SPINACI
Pasta Rolls Stuffed with Spinach and Ricotta Cheese

A delicate dish that we served as a vegetable course...but one that makes a wonderful vegetarian entree.

1 recipe BASIC EGG PASTA
3 tablespoons Butter
½ cup minced fresh Onion
1 10-ounce package frozen Chopped Spinach, defrosted
1 15-ounce tub Ricotta Cheese
2 Eggs, beaten
¼ cup Bread Crumbs
⅛ teaspoon Nutmeg
Salt and freshly ground Pepper to taste
1 cup SALSA DI POMODORO
1 cup BALSAMELLA

Set the pasta dough aside to rest at room temperature for 30 minutes. Melt the butter in a large skillet over medium heat, and saute the onion until transparent. Squeeze all the water you can out of the spinach, and add it to the skillet. Continue to saute for 5 minutes longer. Remove from the heat, and add the ricotta cheese, eggs, bread crumbs, nutmeg, salt and pepper...mix well. Roll out the some of the pasta dough into a sheet that measures 4 inches X 18 inches. Cut the strip into 3 equal rectangles (4 inches X 6 inches). Lay them on a clean, dry counter top. Using a spatula, spread them with the spinach/ricotta cheese mixture (about ¼ inch thick). Spread as smoothly and evenly as you can. Roll up the pasta "jelly roll style" so that you end up with a 4 inch long roll that is about 2 inches in diameter. Roll each pasta roll in microwave-safe plastic wrap...fastening the ends with twist-ties. When you have them all assembled, drop them in simmering water for 12 to 14 minutes. Meanwhile, combine the SALSA DI POMODORO and the BALSAMELLA...heat thoroughly. When the pasta rolls are done, remove them from the simmering water using tongs. Remove the twist-ties and the plastic wrap. Slice into rounds (about ¾ inch thick) and arrange them on a warm platter. Top with sauce. Serve hot.

SPECIAL TIP: You'll have more pasta than you need for this recipe...why not make the rest of the dough into fettucine or linguini. If you let it air dry for 2 to 3 hours, it will keep indefinitely. Then you can have delicate homemade pasta right at your fingertips!

STORAGE INFORMATION: The pasta rolls can be made up to a day ahead and stored (wrapped in the plastic wrap) in the refrigerator until just before serving time.

PREPARATION TIME: 1½ hours

YIELD: 8 servings

COSCIA DI AGNELLO RIPIENA
Stuffed Leg of Lamb

If you like lamb...you'll LOVE this recipe. If you think you DON'T like lamb...you may be surprised! Just make sure that the lamb is young and fresh, and you'll be amazed at the delicate flavor. The stuffing works equally well with beef!

1 Leg of Lamb (about 6 to 8 pounds)
6 ounces Prosciutto, sliced wafer thin
1 large Carrot, shredded very thin
1 small Onion, shredded very thin
Sprinkling of Ground Cloves
Sprinkling of Garlic Powder
A few Grindings of Black Pepper

Begin by boning the leg of lamb. With a sharp knife, cut into the lamb, down to the bone, in the place on the leg where the bone is closest to the surface. Then, using the tip of the knife, seperate the meat from the bone with a scraping action, keeping it all in once piece. Once the bone is removed, trim away any fat you can find. One of the reasons that lamb sometimes has a strong flavor, is that the fat retains much of that objectionable odor. If you trim most, or all of the fat away, it not only tastes better, but lowers the amount of cholesterol in the finished dish. When the roast is trimmed out, lie it flat on a cutting board and cover it with plastic wrap. Pound it (fairly sharply) with a wooded mallet or other blunt object. Place the prosciutto on top of the roast in a single layer. Then add the carrot and the onion. Top with the cloves and garlic and finish with the black pepper. Roll the roast up and tie it securely with kitchen twine. (Having a helper for this portion of the job, is a great advantage!) Place the roast in a pre-heated 375 degree oven for about 1 hour and 15 minutes, or until the internal temperature reaches 145 degrees (medium-rare). Slice the lamb and serve warm.

SPECIAL TIP: An easy way to tie up the roast is with a product that the butcher shops use called "Jet Net". Ask your butcher if you can buy a piece of it for your roast. It is an elastic netting that will hold a rolled roast firmly in place, and then can simply be cut away with a sharp knife prior to slicing.

STORAGE INFORMATION: I like to make rolled roasts up ahead of time and freeze them. They will keep for up to 6 months in the freezer, and then all you need to do is defrost and roast them as usual.

PREPARATION TIME: Less than 2 hours (including roasting time)

YIELD: 6 to 8 servings

I Contorni

Pasta, Rice and Vegetables

SLEIGH BELLS

Our first winter at the lodge was a snowy one. We were so enthralled with the beauty of our canyon, wrapped in ermine and covered with diamonds, that we decided to create the most romantic horse-drawn sleigh ride ever.

We found a wagon maker in Montana who said he could find us a carriage we could put runners under in the winter, and wheels in summer. We commissioned him to build one for us that would carry 12 people plus driver and "shotgun".

Next, we had to find, buy, and learn to harness and drive a team of Belgian draft horses. We found a teamster, whose father had worked the Yellowstone carriages, and who had followed in his father's footsteps. He agreed to sell us a matched team he had trained, and teach us the art of harnessing and driving. His ranch was on the other side of the Big Horn Mountains near Sheridan, Wyoming.

The next summer was very busy indeed, what with working our lodge from mid-week until Monday mornings, then racing over the mountains for two days of schooling, and racing home to get ready for another feast. By late summer we were ready to bring our team home.

We rented an old wagon on rubber tires to con-

tinue working with our Belgian team, named "Bonnie and Clyde", so they could become familiar with all the new sights and sounds . . . and wildlife . . . along the road into our lodge. Our new carriage was scheduled for completion by 1st December.

As winter approached our excitement and confidence grew. Bonnie and Clyde were fat and happy in their new home, responded beautifully to our touch on the reins, and no longer spooked at the game . . . tho their ears showed they knew exactly where every creature was in the canyon.

Finally the big day arrived. We borrowed a friend's flatbed trailer to bring home our beautiful new carriage. What fun to watch the faces along the main streets of the little towns we passed thru on our way home . . . everyone loves a new carriage!

Then the fun was over. The flatbed trailer was too wide to cross the first bridge. The carriage was on its summer wheels. Simple enough, then, to unload it in the campground and pull it into the lodge with the Suburban.

Over the bridge and thru the meadow to the cliffs . . . so far, so good. We started up the steep slope that winds its way over the cliffs guarding the entrance to the canyon. Near the top, the Suburban's wheels spun in the loose gravel. We didn't have enough momentum to make it over the top, so we had to back down all the way to the meadow.

The tongue of the carriage is a full nine feet long to accommodate the big draft horses. The road is one lane with a sheer cliff above and a 150 foot drop below. Backing down was high adventure. Racing back up the slope was exciting too, for near the crest our beautiful new carriage tipped up on two wheels and very nearly ended up in the bottom of the canyon.

After cutting some low hanging limbs that threatened to pierce the high fringed surrey top, we made it all the way in to the corrals. We harnessed the team which promptly balked at the prospect of being hitched to this unfamiliar wagon. Eventually they decided it was okay . . . three days later.

Finally there was enough snow to put the carriage on its runners. Bonnie and Clyde decided it wasn't the same outfit, so we had to introduce them to it all over again.

The first officially scheduled sleigh ride sold out completely. When the big day arrived, the temperature was 10 below zero. Never mind, we had lots of blankets, two thermos jugs of hot chocolate, and hot spiced wine.

The night was overcast, obscuring the moon and stars . . . it was "blacker than the inside of a cow". Never mind, we had a big nine volt flashlight and besides, horses can see in the dark, can't they?

Nearing the crest of the narrow road over the cliffs, Bonnie and Clyde couldn't pull the loaded wagon over the top. Never mind, "Everybody pile out and follow behind 'til we get over the top, okay?".

One hour and ten minutes later, after four more "everybody-pile-out-and-follow-behinds", we reached the lodge. The fire had burned out in the fireplace and the cookstove was cold. Nancy got the fires going again and gave everybody drinks on the house, while I unhitched the team and took them back to the corrals.

The first officially scheduled sleigh ride was also the last. There never came another night that winter when we had enough snow to cover the bare spots, enough moonlight to see, and temperatures warm enough to avoid frostbite. In the spring we sold the whole outfit to the local Budweiser distributor. But, it must have been a great idea, for six years later our patrons are still asking if we do the sleigh rides!

BASIC EGG PASTA

Making pasta is VERY rewarding...and much easier than many would have you think! The moisture content is, by far, the most critical factor. But if you add the water slowly...give the dough time to react... (particularly if you are using the Food Processor Method)...and let the dough "rest"...the results are wonderful!

4 cups All Purpose Flour
4 Extra Large Eggs
1½ Teaspoons Salt
2 Tablespoons Olive Oil
6 to 8 Tablespoons Water

BY HAND: Place all the flour on a clean, dry countertop, making a well in the center. In the well, place the eggs, salt, olive oil and a few tablespoons of the water. Begin mixing with a fork, drawing more flour in from the edges...gradually incorporating all of the ingredients. Add more water as needed to make a stiff (BUT NOT STICKY) dough. Knead for a few minutes, until a smooth ball is formed.

FOOD PROCESSOR METHOD: Place all the ingredients EXCEPT WATER in the work bowl of a food processor fitted with a steel blade.. Process for 30 seconds, or until the mixture resembles corn meal. With the machine running, drizzle water thru the feed tube A TABLESPOON AT A TIME, until the mixture begins to cling together. Remove the lid, and check the moisture content. The dough should come together when pressed with your finger...but just barely feel damp. Add more water and reprocess if needed. If too moist, add a tablespoon or two of flour and reprocess until the proper consistancy is reached. Remove lid and empty the mixture onto a clean, dry countertop. Bring the mixture together into a ball with your hands, and knead until a smooth ball is formed.

TO FINISH: Wrap the dough in plastic wrap, and let rest for 30 minutes or more.

FOR CUT PASTA: Roll out thin sheets of dough either by hand with a rolling pin, or with a pasta machine. Let the sheets air-dry on clean, dry towels for a few minutes, then cut to desired width and air-dry on racks...or cook and serve fresh.

FOR FILLED PASTA: Make one sheet at a time and fill as desired. Do not allow to dry before stuffing. Brush the area of the pasta around the stuffing with beaten egg before closing, to insure a good seal.

VARIATIONS: Whole Wheat Pasta...substitute 2 cups of whole wheat flour for the same amount of all purpose flour and proceed as usual. Spinach Pasta... cook and drain one half a 10-ounce package of frozen chopped spinach according to package directions. Squeeze as much of the moisture out of the pasta as you can and add it to the remaining ingredients...proceed as usual. Herb Pasta...Add 2 teaspoons of one of your favorite dried herbs (Basil, Parsley,

Oregano, Thyme, etc.) and proceed as usual. Chocolate Pasta...add ¼ cup unsweetened baking cocoa...proceed as usual.

STORAGE INFORMATION: Place dried pasta in plastic containers and store in the pantry. Keeps almost indefinitely. Place fresh and/or filled pastas in plastic containers and freeze up to 1 month.

PREPARATION TIME: 1½ hours

YIELD: 10 to 12 servings

RISOTTO

A VERY traditional dish found all over Northern Italy, the basic recipe never varies! But, OH what you can do with that basic recipe!

4 tablespoons Butter
4 tablespoons Olive Oil
1 medium Onion, chopped
1½ cups uncooked Arborio Rice
5 cups of Chicken (or beef) Broth
Salt to taste

In a large skillet, melt the butter and olive oil over medium heat. Saute the onion until transparent. Add the uncooked rice and stir well to coat...sauteing for a few moments. Have the broth simmering in a pan on the back burner. Add a ladle or two of the broth to the rice, quickly stiring to incorporate. When that broth has been absorbed, add another ladle full and then another, until the rice is done.

VARIATIONS: Add a few grains of golden saffron and ½ cup of white wine, and you have Risotto alla Milanese. For Risotto con Funghi, just add 5 or 6 thinly sliced mushrooms...or, add 1 cup of fresh or frozen green peas, and you have Risotto con Piselli!

SPECIAL TIP: A good test for doneness, is to bite into an individual grain of rice. It should be creamy on the outside, but still be firm on the inside!

STORAGE INFORMATION: Cook and serve immediately, or UNDER cook and store in the refrigerator...finishing just before serving.

PREPARATION TIME: 40 minutes

YIELD: 6 servings

POLENTA

A traditional and versatile dish, Polenta is made from coarse corn meal, salt and water, and generally served as an accompaniement to roast meats, with some of the sauce spooned over the top! But, OH! the many things you can do with Polenta. There are appetizers, such as POLENTA ALLA LODIGIANA (included in this book), and even a Polenta cheesecake! Another great way to serve Polenta, is simply sliced and fried in butter. (Mr. B and I "American-ize" our left-over Polenta, by serving it fried, and topped with warm maple syrup with a few sausages on the side as a wonderful Sunday brunch!)

6 cups Water
1½ teaspoons Coarse Salt
1½ cups Coarse Polenta (or coarse Corn Meal)

Bring the water to a rolling boil in a large saucepan over high heat on the stovetop. Slowly add the polenta (or corn meal)...being very careful not to inter-upt the boiling. Once all the meal has been incorporated to the water, add the salt. Continue to boil stirring constantly until done (45 minutes to 1 hour). Mean-while, keep a small pan of simmering water on the back burner, and add extra water as needed. The Polenta will thicken rather quickly, and may appear to be done. But, it must cook for at least 45 minutes...and the longer you can cook it, the creamier it will become. When it is done, it will be extremely thick...as a matter of fact, you should literally be able to stand a spoon in it without it falling over! Depending on how you plan to serve it, you can either pour it out of the pan into a free-form round onto a cutting board, or platter...or pour it into a mold for slicing and frying later.

SPECIAL TIPS: It is very important NOT to interupt the boiling when making Polenta. It tends to make the Polenta seperate, and the quality is not as good. When adding the polenta or corn meal to the boiling water...take your time! Also, using a wire whip for this part of the process, will help avoid lumps! Once in the pan, you can switch to a nice heavy spoon.

STORAGE INFORMATION: Keeps very well refrigerated for 4 to 5 days. DO NOT FREEZE...the water seperates from the corn meal, and it resembles a rub-ber sponge!!!

PREPARATION TIME: 1 hour

YIELD: 8 servings

GNOCCHI ALLA ROMANA
Roman Semolino Dumplings

A wonderfully creamy and satisfying addition to any meal...the perfect accompaniment to CROCCHETTE DI POLLO.

2¼ cups Whole Milk
1 cup Semolino Flour
2 Egg Yolks
¼ cup Butter (½ stick)
¾ cup grated Parmesan Cheese
Salt to taste
2 tablespoons additional melted Butter
¼ cup grated Parmesan Cheese

In a large sauce pan, bring the milk to a near simmer over medium heat. Gradually add the semolino, while stirring with a wire whisk to avoid lumps. As soon as all the semolino is incorporated, use a large spoon to stir the mixture, as it will quickly get too thick for the whisk to handle. Continue to cook, stirring constantly, for about 15 to 20 minutes. Remove the pan from the heat and immediately add the egg yolks, butter and the cheese. Stir briskly to blend well. Line a jelly roll pan with plastic wrap, and empty the hot mixture into it. Using a spatula, distribute the mixture as evenly as you can. Then top the mixture with another layer of plastic wrap and, being careful not to burn yourself, use your hands to flatten the mixture to about ⅜ inch thick. Let the mixture cool completely. Using a biscuit cutter, or a small glass, cut the cooled dough into rounds. Place them in a buttered baking dish so that they slightly overlap. Drizzle with the melted butter, and top with the remaining cheese. Bake at 400 degrees for about 20 minutes, or until lightly golden brown. Serve hot.

SPECIAL TIP: Dip the cutter in water before cutting each round and they won't stick to it.

STORAGE INFORMATION: Before baking, the gnocchi can be placed on a wax paper lined tray, covered with plastic wrap and quick frozen. Then, just gather them up and store them in a plastic bag. Defrost and bake as usual.

PREPARATION TIME: 40 minutes

YIELD: 6 servings

ZUCCHINE AL FORNO
Baked Zucchine

So delightfully simple, you'll want to serve this dish often...especially when zucchine is taking over your garden! A tasty accompaniment to meat, fish or fowl...or a flavorful vegetarian entree!

2 medium-size fresh Zucchine
3 or 4 tablespoons Bread Crumbs
3 or 4 tablespoons grated Parmesan Cheese
2 tablespoons Olive Oil
Salt and freshly ground Black Pepper to taste

Wash the zucchine and slice them on the diagonal into ¼" thick slices. Place them in an oiled oven-proof baking dish, overlapping the slices, and arranging them in an attractive pattern. Distribute the bread crumbs evenly over the top...then the Parmesan. Drizzle the olive oil over all, topped with a sprinkling of salt and a few grindings of pepper. Place the baking dish in a preheated 375 degree oven for about 15 minutes, or until the zucchine are golden brown on top.

STORAGE INFORMATION: Assemble this dish up to several hours before serving. DO NOT FREEZE.

PREPARATION TIME: 10 minutes, plus baking time.

YIELD: 4 servings

CAROTE ALLA CREMA
Carrots in Cream Sauce

As simple a dish as you will find…which gives it it's elegance!

1 pound medium size fresh Carrots
2 tablespoons Butter
¾ cup Heavy Whipping Cream
Salt and White Pepper to taste
Dash of Nutmeg

Peel the carrots and slice them approximately ⅛ inch thick. Cook the carrots in boiling, salted water for about 3 minutes, or until "tender crisp". Drain and set aside. Melt the butter in a large skillet and saute the carrots for 1 minute…then add the cream. Boil rapidly for 3 to 4 minutes to "reduce" the sauce. Add salt, white pepper (a tiny dash will do!) and nutmeg to taste. Serve very hot. This dish goes particularly well with MAIALE ARROSTO AFFETATO, or any roast or grilled meat that is served without a sauce of its' own.

STORAGE INFORMATION: The carrots can be par-boiled several hours in advance and the dish "finished" just before serving.

PREPARATION TIME: 15 to 20 minutes

YIELD: 4 to 6 servings

VERDURE E FORMAGGIO AL FORNO
Baked Vegetables with Cheese

A remarkable summertime dish! So simple...so few ingredients...yet a delicious combination that will delight your family!

2 cups fresh Zucchine, sliced very thin
1 small Onion, minced
3 large, red, ripe Tomatoes, seeded and diced
2 Anchovy Filets, cut into tiny pieces
6 ounces grated Asiago Cheese
(a Sharp White New York Cheddar makes a reasonable substitute)
3 tablespoons dry Bread Crumbs
¼ cup Extra Virgin Olive Oil
Freshly ground Black Pepper to taste

Distribute the zucchine, the onion and the tomatoes over the bottom of a flat, oven-proof baking dish. Dot the top with the bits of anchovy...then top with the grated cheese. Sprinkle the bread crumbs over all...then drizzle the olive oil evenly over the surface, followed by a generous grinding of black pepper. Place the dish in a preheated 400 degree oven for 15 minutes, or until the cheese is a light, golden brown. Serve hot.

SPECIAL TIP: Don't cheat yourself out of a special taste treat by omitting the anchovies. We served it here at the lodge and most people didn't even know that they were there! They do add a depth of flavor that it quite unexpected. If you simply CAN'T do anchovies...you'll need to add a little salt in their place. But DO try it...you'll LIKE it!

STORAGE INFORMATION: Assemble several hours in advance and store in the refrigerator (covered) until just before serving time.

PREPARATION TIME: 30 minutes

YIELD: 4 servings

CIPOLLE E CAROTE FRITTE
Batter-fried Onions and Carrots

This is a wonderful recipe! The beer batter works well not only with carrots and onions, but just about any of your favorite vegetables! Serve them as an appetizer, or as an accompaniment to a dish such as BISTECCA ALLA FIORENTINE! Fabulous!

4 large Carrots (or 6 medium)
2 small Yellow Onions
1 cup Flour
¾ cup Dark Italian Beer (German beer will do, of course)
2 Eggs, beaten
1 tablespoon Olive Oil
Pinch of Salt
Vegetable Oil for deep frying
Salt to taste

Peel the carrots and slice them on the diagonal into ⅛ inch thick slices. Peel the onions and slice them into wedges about 1 inch across at the widest part. Skewer two pieces of the onion and one slice of the carrot onto toothpicks. Set aside while you prepare the batter. Combine the next five ingredients in a medium size bowl, and whisk with a wire whip. Heat about 2 inches of the oil in a heavy pan (or a deep fryer, if you have one) until it reaches 375 degrees. Dip the vegetables into the batter and drop them into the hot oil...frying them a few at a time, until they are a deep golden brown. Remove them from the oil with a slotted spoon and place them onto paper towels to drain. Salt to taste. Keep them hot in a 250 degree oven while you deep fry the rest. Serve hot.

STORAGE INFORMATION: The skewers can be made up several hours in advance, and stored in the refrigerator in a plastic bag. Just dip them into the batter and fry as usual.

PREPARATION TIME: 30 minutes

YIELD: 24 appetizers

FUNGHI TRIFOLATI
Mushrooms sauteed like Truffles

The extraordinary flavor of wild mushrooms elevates this simple dish into another realm. A great accompaniment to roast or broiled meats...like BISTECCA ALLA FIORENTINA.

2 ounces dried Porcini Mushrooms
(Shitake Mushrooms may be substituted, if need be)
2 pounds fresh domestic Mushrooms, sliced as thinly as possible
½ cup (1 stick) Butter
½ cup Marsala Wine Salt and freshly ground Pepper to taste

Soak the dried Porcini in 1½ cups of boiling water for 15 to 20 minutes, or until they are very soft. Line a collander or seive with a paper towel, and place it in a bowl. Pour the mushrooms (with the water) into the seive, straining the broth, and reserving it for later. Remove the paper towel from the seive, and rinse the mushrooms with hot running water. Wild mushrooms generally contain a lot of sand. This will remove the sand, and yet still let you use the wonderful broth for added flavor...not grit! Melt the butter in a large skillet, and begin sauteeing the fresh mushrooms until they are limp. Add the Porcini, the broth and the Marsala wine. Simmer over medium heat for several minutes until all the liquid is evaporated. Add salt and pepper to taste. Continue sauteing, until the mushrooms begin to lightly brown. Serve hot.

STORAGE INFORMATION: Have the Porcini ready, and the fresh mushrooms sliced, and just saute before serving.

PREPARATION TIME: 30 minutes

YIELD: 4 servings

CIPOLLINE IN AGRODOLCE
Sweet and Sour Little Onions

A most unusual dish, and one that will certainly dazzle your guests or family! This exciting dish goes well with most roast meats...but my favorite is MAIALE ARROSTO AFFETATO.

2 10-ounce or 1 16-ounce package frozen Little Onions
(defrosted and drained)
¼ cup Butter
¼ cup Brown Sugar (packed)
¼ cup Red Wine Vinegar
Salt to taste

Melt butter in a large skillet. When butter foams, add drained onions. Saute over medium heat for 5 to 8 minutes, or until onions begin to turn color. Add brown sugar, and stir to coat onions. Add vinegar, and simmer 2 to 3 minutes longer. Sauce should be thick enough to coat onions well. Salt to taste.

SPECIAL TIP: If you're in a hurry, a brief visit to the microwave or a dunk in a bowl of hot water, will do the defrosting for you!

STORAGE INFORMATION: This is best when made fresh just before serving...and it's so quick and easy, there's no need to prepare ahead!

PREPARATION TIME: 20 minutes.

YIELD: 4 to 6 servings

105

FUNGHI IN FRICASSEA
Sauteed Mushrooms with Egg and Lemon Sauce

An easy and unusual dish...this one's guaranteed to draw rave reviews!

2 pounds fresh Mushrooms, cleaned and sliced
4 tablespoons (½ stick) Butter
Salt and Pepper to taste

For the Sauce:

1 tablespoon Butter
1 tablespoon Flour
1 Egg Yolk
1 cup Chicken Broth
2 tablespoons Lemon Juice
Salt and Pepper to taste

In a large skillet, saute the mushrooms in the butter, adding salt and pepper to suit your own taste. Meanwhile, make the sauce. Melt the butter in a small skillet and stir in the flour. Quickly whisk in the remaining ingredients with a wire whisk. Simmer over medium heat for several minutes. If the sauce is too thick, thin it with a little more of the broth. If it is too thin, simply continue to simmer to reduce the sauce to the desired consistancy. When the mushrooms begin to lightly brown, serve hot, topped with sauce.

SPECIAL TIPS: Water is the number one enemy of fresh mushrooms! When you buy fresh mushrooms at the store, put them directly into a PAPER bag...NOT PLASTIC! The condensation will result in slimy mushrooms in a day or so! Paper will absorb the condensation and prolong the life of the mushrooms. Also...don't WASH mushrooms, just wipe excess dirt from them with paper towels.

STORAGE INFORMATION: The sauce can be made a day ahead and re-heated. Otherwise, make and serve immediately.

PREPARATION TIME: 30 minutes

YIELD: 4 to 6 servings

VERDURE AL CARTOCCIO
Vegetables Baked in Parchment

A delightful way to cook and serve vegetables! It not only steams them to tender perfection, but captures the nutrients in the parchemnt envelope!

2 10-ounce packages frozen Vegetable
(Broccoli Spears, Asparagus Spears, Green Beans, etc.)
6 tablespoons Butter, melted
6 slices fresh Lemon (approximately ¼" thick)
Salt to taste
Baking Parchment

Defrost the vegetables to room temperature. Cut the baking parchment into squares approximately 10" X 10". On each square, place 3 to 4 ounces of the vegetable. Top with a tablespoon of the melted butter, a sprinkling of salt, and a lemon slice. Bringing the sides of the parchment up, seal the packet as tightly as you can, and tuck the ends underneath. Place the packets on a baking sheet, and bake in a preheated 400 degree oven for 25 minutes. Serve by opening the packet slightly to allow the steam to escape and let the pretty colors of the lemon and the vegetables tantalize your guests!

STORAGE INFORMATION: The packets can be made up several hours in advance, and stored in the refrigerator until just before serving time. Then, time the baking to coincide with the rest of your meal!

PREPARATION TIME: 40 minutes

YIELD: 4 to 6 servings

TORTELLINI DI PREZZEMOLO E FORMAGGIO
Tortellini filled with Parsley and Cheese

Hand made tortellini are reserved for very special occasions! They do take some time to make, but Oh Boy!...are they worth the effort! Here we offer a recipe for tortellini filled with Parsley and a blend of Ricotta and Parmesan Cheeses...topped with SALSA ALFREDO!

1 recipe BASIC EGG PASTA (or Spinach Pasta, if you prefer)
⅓ cup finely chopped fresh Parsley
1-15-ounce container Ricotta Cheese
1 cup grated Parmesan Cheese
½ teaspoon Salt
1 Egg Yolk
¼ teaspoon Nutmeg
1 recipe of SALSA ALFREDO

Combine the parsley, ricotta, Parmesan, salt, egg yolk and nutmeg in a bowl...mixing well. Roll a small amount of the pasta dough into a very thin sheet, keeping the rest of the dough in a plastic bag. (You'll want to fill all the tortellini you cut from this sheet before you roll out another, so as to avoid having the dough dry out!) Cut the dough into circles about 2 to 2 ¼ inches in diameter. Place about ½ teaspoon of the cheese/parsley mixture in the center of each circle. Fold the circle in half and seal. Bend the tortellini around the tip of your index finger...firmly pressing one corner over the other to fasten them together. Place the tortellini on clean, dry towels, until all are completed. Make the SALSA ALFREDO according to the recipe...keeping it warm until serving time. Bring a large pot of water to a boil on high heat. Drop the tortellini into the water a few at a time. Fresh tortellini only take 2 to 3 minutes to cook...so be careful not to over cook them! Drain the tortellini, and put them in a buttered dish warmed in the oven. Top with SALSA ALFREDO, a little chopped Parsley and grated Parmesan cheese...serve hot.

SPECIAL TIP: If you're having trouble getting a good seal on the tortellini, dip a pastry brush in water (shake off the excess) and lightly brush the surface of the pasta before stuffing and sealing.

STORAGE INFORMATION: The tortellini can be made several hours in advance of cooking. Just place them on a baking sheet lined with a towel, cover them with plastic wrap, and refrigerate. (DO NOT FREEZE) Make up the sauce ahead, too! Then, just heat the sauce...cook the tortellini and serve!

PREPARATION TIME: 1 hour

YIELD: 6 servings

VENISON SALAD

The lodge is half way between the equator and the north pole . . . just south of the 45th parallel . . . and 6,400 feet above sea level. According to all the experts, we may expect 54 frost free growing days. In six years, the most we've ever had is 37.

Whenever possible, Nancy cooks with fresh herbs. She even has her own Bay Leaf tree. It was inevitable that we would build a green house so she could have her herbs.

The first one was very small and built with scrap lumber, used sprinkler parts, and glassed over with old storm windows and plastic. It worked just great the first couple of years. Thereafter, Nancy announced it no

longer filled her needs, and I was to build her a bigger one.

The bigger one was five times as big, and built from a redwood kit we bought thru the mail from a company in Santa Barbara, California. We went from a Model "T" to a Cadillac overnight.

We have a long range plan, of sorts, for our canyon home. It includes expanding the grassy areas, clearing the underbrush and deadfalls, getting more of the creek water to the natural trees and shrubs that live here . . . and building and planting flower/herb gardens here and there to complement the beauty of the wilderness.

The flower/herb garden aspect of our long range plan was immediately shifted to top priority, and shortly thereafter, into total panic.

As all new owners of BIG greenhouses can tell you, there are two lessons to be learned the hard way. First, surely there is more room than will ever be used . . . wrong! And second . . . may as well plant the rest of the seeds in the packet since we have all this room . . . wrong! These two misconceptions combine to create an explosive force.

Even with drastic thinning and foisting plants on all our friends, the greenhouse was soon bursting at the seams. With no alternative, we had to put plants out early, knowing full well many would not survive the late frosts.

One benefit of that first experience . . . we learned which bedding plants and herbs could withstand the late frosts.

There's another hazard to gardening that exists in this geographic location . . . wildlife. The deer present the greatest threat, by way of sheer tenacity, but also the moose and elk, if the winter is quite severe.

Nancy declared war on the deer in short order. It seems delphinium, chive, broadleaf parsley, oregano . . . not to mention thyme and mountain harebell . . . combine to make the finest tossed salad any deer ever dreamed of finding in a lifetime!

By trial and error, she discovered which herbs and bedding plants were favorites of the deer, and placed them closest to the buildings. That worked for awhile . . . kind of! Then she took to setting the sprinklers going during the deer's favorite feeding times. That worked for awhile, too . . . kind of!

What really saved Nancy's gardens, for the most part, was providence. Our busiest season coincides with the 35-40 frost free days we are supposed to have each year. The activity on our road, around the buildings and on the hillside trails, worked together to keep the deer at bay.

A truce of sorts has evolved between Nancy and the deer. She builds an impenetrable hardware cloth cage around and over the raspberry patch. She also plants lots of extras of everything in the forlorn belief they will overeat and decide they don't like this one or that one. It does take them longer so, to the extent Nancy has more time to shoo them away, it's beneficial.

The bottom line, though, is that as soon as they start showing up in late summer, Nancy starts frantically harvesting all their favorite herbs and puts out whatever she has left of those bedding plants they dislike. All the while the deer gather round watching her every move and look sorrowfully at her with their big soft brown eyes. I've caught her more than once overlooking a bit of thyme here and a patch of chive there. Do you suppose she's weakening?

INSALATA DI PASTA PRIMAVERA DELLA CASA
Spring Pasta Salad alla Brannon's

Choose carefully the time of the year when you serve this salad, and take advantage of the wonderful fresh vegetables when they are at the height of their season! It makes a lovely luncheon entree, as well as a salad following a light meal.

1 cup Broccoli Flowerettes, blanched
1 cup fresh Asparagus Spears cut into 1 inch strips, blanched
½ cup shredded fresh Carrots
1 cup diced fresh Tomato
1 bunch Green Onions, sliced
1 Sweet Red Pepper, seeded and coarsely chopped
¼ cup Pignoli (Pine Nuts)
8 to 10 OLIVE MARINATE
¼ pound Vermicelli, broken into 2" lengths, cooked al dente
3 tablespoons White Wine Vinegar
⅓ cup Extra Virgin Olive Oil
2 tablespoons Heavy Whipping Cream
1 tablespoon DiJon-type Mustard
Garlic Salt and freshly ground Black Pepper to taste
½ cup freshly grated Parmesan Cheese

Blanch the broccoli flowerettes and the asparagus pieces by dropping them into boiling water. Bring the water back up to a boil and cook the vegetables for 3 or 4 minutes, or until tender-crisp. Drain them in a colander, and then plunge them immediately into ice cold water to stop the cooking, and preserve the bright green color. Combine all the vegetables, the pignoli, the olives and the vermicelli in a large salad bowl. Whisk the remaining ingredients (except the Parmesan) in a small bowl and then pour the mixture over the salad. Toss well. Serve the salad at room temperature mounded on a crisp lettuce leaf, topped with grated Parmesan.

SPECIAL TIP: Pasta that is made with all purpose flour is not sturdy enough to withstand being tossed in a salad...that's why I recommend a commercial pasta made with durham wheat or semolino. You can use most any type you like...from vermicelli or spaghetti to tiny pasta shells or spirals!

STORAGE INFORMATION: This dish will keep refrigerated for several hours before serving...but in order to keep the nice bright colors, don't dress the salad until a few minutes prior to serving time.

PREPARATION TIME: 30 minutes

YIELD: 6 servings

INSALATA BISTECCA
Steak Salad

A fabulous Summer luncheon entree...wait for the right season, when you can grill the steak outdoors, and the tomatoes are a deep, deep red! And...it's a delicious way to use up that left-over steak from last night's backyard barbeque!

2 pounds Sirloin Steak, charcoal broiled to medium rare
1 pound fresh Mushrooms, sliced very thin
1 bunch Green Onions, cleaned and sliced
2 large ripe Tomatoes, diced
2 tablespoons fresh Parsley, chopped
½ cup Extra Virgin Olive Oil
3 tablespoons Red Wine Vinegar
2 tablespoons DiJon-type Mustard
Garlic Salt and freshly ground Black Pepper to taste
1 large head of Romaine or Leaf Lettuce, shredded

Chill the cooked steak, and slice it on the diagonal, VERY THIN. Place the steak slices in a bowl with the mushrooms, green onions, tomatoes and parsley. Add the olive oil, vinegar, and mustard, tossing well. Then, season with garlic salt and freshly ground pepper to taste. Refrigerate up to two hours before serving. Mound the salad on a bed of the shredded lettuce and serve.

STORAGE INFORMATION: Have the steak grilled and stored in the refrigerator for up to 3 days ahead. Then just finshed the assembly 2 hours before serving time.

PREPARATION TIME: 40 minutes

YIELD: 4 servings

INSALATA RUSSA
Russian Salad

In Italy, anything that's a real mess, or loosely put together, is called "a real Russia"! Therefore they call this mixed vegetable salad INSALATA RUSSA.

1 cup Green Peas, (fresh or frozen), cooked
1 cup Green Beans (fresh or frozen), cooked
1 large, fresh Carrot, diced and cooked
1 8-ounce can Diced Beets
1 large Russet Potato, boiled, skinned and diced
½ cup thinly sliced fresh Celery
1 small Red Onion, coarsely chopped
½ to ¾ cup MAIONESE AL' LIMONE
Salt and Freshly Ground Black Pepper
Grated peel of 1 Lemon

When cooking the peas, green beans and carrots, UNDER COOK them. They should be "tender crisp". Then plunge them into cold water to stop the cooking process. Drain them thoroughly...taking care to get them as dry as you can. Excess moisture on the vegetables will only water down the wonderful flavor of the lemon mayonaise! It's an especially good idea to rinse the beets well, before adding them to the salad. They are going to turn the salad very pink as it is! Rinsing will keep the effect to a minimum. Combine all of the ingredients...adding salt and pepper to taste.

SPECIAL TIP: The salad should be allowed to marinate for a few hours before serving. When you're ready to present it to your guests, taste it again. You may want to adjust the salt and pepper one last time.

STORAGE INFORMATION: Will keep nicely for several days in a covered container in the refrigerator.

PREPARATION TIME: 30 minutes

YIELD: 4 to 6 servings

INSALATA DI ARANCIA
Orange Salad

An unusual combination that becomes an item of conversation...not only because it's so unheard of...but because it's delicious and refreshing!

4 medium Naval Oranges
8 large pitted Green Sicilian Olives
(Spanish Olives with the pimentos removed will do)
2 tablespoons Extra Virgin Olive Oil
1 tablespoon White Wine Vinegar
Salt and Pepper to taste

With a very sharp knife, cut the rind from the orange, including the white, pithy part. Slice the orange into ¼ inch rounds and place them in a large bowl. Slice the olives and add them to the bowl. Drizzle the olive oil and the white wine vinegar over the top and toss well. Add salt and pepper to taste. Refrigerate (covered) until serving time. Serve chilled.

STORAGE INFORMATION: Make several hours before serving time and store in a covered plastic container.

PREPARATION TIME: 15 minutes

YIELD: 4 servings

INSALATA DI CAVOLO ROSSO ALLA TORINESE
Red Cabbage Salad in the style of Turin

A dish known only to the Northern town of Turin, this unusual salad is beautiful, as well as flavorful!

1 medium head of Red Cabbage
1 recipe of BAGNA CAUDA

Shred the cabbage as finely as you can. (Don't grate or chop.) Have the cabbage at room temperature, stored in a bowl covered with plastic wrap. About 10 minutes before serving time, make the BAGNA CAUDA, and pour it over the cabbage, tossing to mix well. Serve at room temperature.

SPECIAL TIP: Follow this course with a palate cleanser such as GRANITA DI LIMONE O LIMETTA. While the flavor of the BAGNA CAUDA is fabulous, it IS very heavy on the garlic!

STORAGE INFORMATION: The cabbage can be shredded several hours in advance of serving time, and stored at room temperature. The BAGNA CAUDA can be assembled ahead as well, and simply heated and combined with the cabbage at the last moment.

PREPARATION TIME: 15 minutes

YIELD: 6 servings

INSALATA DI BROCCOLI
Broccoli Salad

A zippy and colorful salad, seasoned with lemon juice and red pepper flakes!

1 head of fresh Broccoli
10 to 12 Pitted Ripe Olives, sliced
⅓ cup Extra Virgin Olive Oil
1 to 2 tablespoons fresh Lemon Juice
Garlic Salt to taste
½ teaspoon Dried Red Pepper Flakes

Remove the flowerettes from the broccoli stems, reserving the stems for another use. Blanche the flowerettes by dropping them into boiling water for 60 seconds...then plunging them into ice cold water for another 60 seconds, or until cool. This will lightly cook them, and bring our the bright green color.

Drizzle the olive oil over the top, followed by the lemon juice and the rest of the ingredients. Stir well to coat the broccoli. Serve chilled, or as the Italians do, at room temperature.

SPECIAL TIP: If you are making this salad a day in advance, wait to "dress" it until a couple of hours ahead of serving time. Otherwise, the color of the broccoli will fade from a bright green to a dull one.

STORAGE INFORMATION: Store in the refrigerator for up to 2 hours before serving time.

PREPARATION TIME: 20 minutes

YIELD: 4 servings

PANZANELLA
Tuscan Bread Salad

As true a "peasant" dish as you'll probably ever find! Generally made in the height of summer, when the fresh vegetables are at their prime, the Tuscans, (true to their sturdy spirit,) make do with the best of WHATEVER the season has to offer! So, feel free to substitute when you get to the produce department! Cherry Tomatoes instead of larger ones...a bit of fresh Broccoli or Cauliflower...whatever suits your fancy! The dressing, however, and the PANE TOSCANO are essential!

¼ to ½ a loaf PANE TOSCANO (Tuscan Bread)

(preperfably "day old")

2 large red ripe Tomatoes

1 Bell Pepper

(green will do...but a Sweet Red or Yellow Pepper is prettier!)

1 small Red Onion

1 large Cucumber

3 or 4 fresh Basil Leaves, finely chopped

(or 1 teaspoon dried Basil)

2 cloves fresh Garlic, minced

Extra Virgin Olive Oil (a good "fruity" one)

(if you must measure...about ½ Cup)

Red Wine Vinegar

(to taste...but about ¼ Cup)

Coarse Salt and Freshly Ground Pepper to taste

Break the bread into large hunks and place them in a bowl...cover with water, and let soak while you prepare the rest of the salad. Cutting right into the bowl, coarsely cut up the vegetables. Add the basil and the garlic. Squeeze all the moisture you can out of the bread with your hands, and crumble it on top of the salad. Next, add the vinegar and oil in a circular motion over the top of the salad. Sprinkle on a little salt and pepper to taste. Let salad sit for 30 minutes before serving. Taste, and if necessary, adjust the seasoning just before serving.

SPECIAL TIP: Enjoy yourself when making this fabulous salad! Don't be intimidated by free-pouring the dressing. When you get used to dressing a salad in this way, you may never buy another BOTTLE of dressing again!

STORAGE INFORMATION: Make up the salad WITHOUT the dressing and place in a covered bowl in the refrigerator until 30 minutes before serving time. Dress...let salad marinate for at least 30 minutes and serve!

PREPARATION TIME: 15 minutes

YIELD: 4 to 6 servings

INSALATA DI FAGIOLI
White Bean Salad

In Central Italy, much use is made of dried beans (legumes) in salads and side dishes. Italians don't eat nearly as much meat as we Americans do, and the beans are a great source of vegetable protein!

1 8-ounce package dried Navy Beans
(soaked overnight and cooked according to package directions)
OR
1 15-ounce can Great Northern Beans (pre-cooked)
' (drained and rinsed)
2 ounces Prosciutto, sliced, then finely chopped (if Prosciutto is unavailable, Boiled Ham can be substituted)
2 tablespoons Black Olives, chopped
2 tablespoons Sun Dried Tomatoes, chopped
½ teaspoon Garlic Salt
1 teaspoon dried Parsley Flakes
Coarse Ground Black Pepper to taste
½ cup Extra Virgin Olive Oil
3 tablespoons White Wine Vinegar

Combine all the ingredients together at least 4 hours before serving. Serve chilled, or at room temperature.

SPECIAL TIP: The beans will absorb a lot of the salt and vinegar during the time before serving, and may not have the "zing" you want. Taste and adjust the seasoning just before you serve. You may want to add more garlic salt, and/or more vinegar!

STORAGE INFORMATION: Keeps several days in the refrigerator.

PREPARATION TIME: 20 minutes (excluding time to soak and cook dried beans)

YIELD: 4 to 6 servings

INSALATA MISTA MARINATA
Marinated Mixed Vegetable Salad

Pick the best that the season has to offer! A crispy, mixed vegetable salad is always a delightful addition to any meal!

3 cups of Fresh Vegetables
⅓ cup Extra Virgin Olive Oil
2 to 3 tablespoons Red Wine Vinegar
Garlic Salt to taste
½ teaspoon dried Basil
Several grindings of Black Pepper

The choice of vegetables is up to you…just use your imagination! You might like to include broccoli, zucchine, red onion, sweet red or yellow peppers, cucumbers, radishes, celery, carrots, turnips, celery root (celeriac), tomatoes…even raw potato! Just keep in mind a balance of color, so that you maximize the "eye-appeal" of this lively salad. Wash and chop the vegetables coarsely, and place them in a large bowl. Drizzle the olive oil over the top, followed by the red wine vinegar and the remaining ingredients. Toss the salad well, and put it into a covered plastic container for a few hours before serving.

VARIATION: If you like, top the salad with a little grated cheese…perhaps Asiago or Parmesan.

STORAGE INFORMATION: Can be made up to a day ahead, and stored (covered) in the refrigerator.

PREPARATION TIME: 20 minutes

YIELD: 4 servings

I Dolci

Desserts

NAKED PHOTOGRAPHER

The main lodge building is dedicated completely to the business. Our home is the chalet . . . with loft bedroom, private bath, kitchen, dinette, and a living room with woodburning stove.

One of the first things we did when we began the restoration of the chalet was remove all the tattered curtains and rods and clean the windows. The view from every window is so spectacular that, to this day, we have never replaced them. In this most remote wilderness, who needs blinds, let alone curtains or drapes?

Nancy and I are both avid photographers. Wildlife in their natural habitat are perhaps our favorite subjects.

When we moved in, the area surrounding the lodge facility was void of all wildlife

. . . including birds and squirrels . . . due, we subsequently learned, to our predecessor's constant target practice with every kind of weapon, and shooting anything that moved.

We cleaned up the underbrush, built a feeder for the birds, put out salt blocks for the elk, deer and moose, and prohibited all use of firearms anywhere in the vicinity of our leasehold . . . more than a half mile of the upper Sweetwater Canyon.

Toward the end of the second year we began to hear birds on the hillsides, and a few even ventured down to investigate our new feeder.

The squirrels were first to come and stay . . . robbing the feeder, chattering at our goings and comings, and finding all the openings in the buildings into which they stuffed their pine cones. I was busied patching openings and building a squirrel shield around the feeder post.

With our binoculars, we began to see elk and bear on the upper slopes. Downstream and upstream we would see deer and moose in the creek bottom. We were encouraged to believe they would soon reclaim our little oasis as their own.

Each morning the first one out of bed would circle the curtainless windows to survey the grounds in hopes of sighting Mr. Bear or Mr. Elk. What a wonderful morning it was when we spotted two cow elk and one calf in the clearing behind the lodge!

As a part of the restoration of the chalet, we built a glassed in porch on the front, with window seats on three sides and, of course, curtains were taboo.

I awoke one morning to Nancy's shriek from downstairs. I knew instantly it was excitement . . . not fright. I grabbed my robe and jumped into my slippers, ran down the stairs from our loft bedroom to find Nancy nowhere in sight. I called to her . . . no answer.

Looking out the nearest window I saw the culmination of all our efforts and patience. The chalet was literally surrounded by a herd of elk munching away on the new spring green lawn...but no sign of Nancy.

I slowly opened the door to the porch, so as not to startle the elk a few feet from the windows, and there was Nancy, trying to be invisible behind the narrow door post, snapping her camera shutter in every direction . . . and . . . naked as a Jaybird!

You see, we sleep in the nude and when, for the first time in your life, you have elk to photograph an arm's length away, who needs a robe?

CROSTATA ALLA CREMA
Custard Tart

A sweet, wholesome desert guaranteed to please young and old alike!

⅔ cup Sugar
6 Egg Yolks
3¾ cup Whole Milk
¾ cup Flour + 3 tablespoons
Rind of 1 Whole Lemon
1 tart shell according PASTA FROLLA I (unbaked)

With an electric mixer, combine the egg yolks and the sugar. Beat at medium speed until frothy. In a large saucepan, combine the flour and milk with a wire whisk, until the flour is completely incorporated into the milk. Peel the whole lemon, as though you would an apple…leaving the rind all in one piece, if possible. Add it to the milk mixture and place it on the stovetop on low/medium heat, until the mixture thickens, and no longer tastes of raw flour. Remove the lemon rind and discard it. With the electric mixer running, add a soup ladle full of the milk mixture to the egg mixture. Stir well. Add another ladle full, and then another, until both mixtures are combined into the larger pan. Pour the custard into a large bowl and cover it with plastic wrap until it cools. Meanwhile, prepare the crust, according to the instructions in PASTA FROLLA I. Pour the cooled custard into the pastry shell and bake it in a preheated 375 degree oven for approximately 30 minutes, or until golden brown. Let cool slightly, and serve warm or, at room temperature. If you like, top each slice with a dollop of freshly whipped cream and a little shaved chocolate.

STORAGE INFORMATION: Keeps well in the refrigerator for up to a week…in the freezer for up to 30 days. Place in a 250 degree oven for 20 to 25 minutes before serving.

PREPARATION TIME: 1 hour

YIELD: 12 servings

RAVIOLI DOLCI DI CIOCCOLATO
Chocolate Ravioli

As strange as it sounds, chocolate pasta is fairly common in parts of Italy. But, they generally serve it with a red sauce, as an entree or a side dish. THIS version, was totally our invention...and, frankly, was a smash hit with our guests!

½ recipe Chocolate Pasta (See BASIC EGG PASTA...variations)
1 15-ounce tub Ricotta Cheese
¼ cup Brown Sugar
6 ounces Nestle's Little Bits (semi-sweet chocolate)
¼ teaspoon Cinnamon
1 Egg, well beaten
Vegetable Oil for deep frying
Powdered Sugar

Let the pasta rest at room temperature for 30 minutes before making your ravioli. Meanwhile, combine the remaining ingredients (except the egg) in a medium size bowl...mixing well. Using a roller-type pasta machine (or a rolling pin), roll the pasta very, very thin. Cut it into 4 inch squares, and place a rounded teaspoon of the filling on top of the pasta square, slightly off center...towards one corner. Brush the edges of the pasta with beaten egg. Fold the square diagonally, so as to make a triangle-shaped ravioli. Crimp with the tines of a fork to seal well. As you complete the raviolis, place them on a clean, dry towel to lightly air dry. In a deep fryer (or a large sauce pan with a heavy bottom), heat the oil to 375 degrees. Fry the raviolis a few at a time. They will get quite puffy. When they begin to lightly brown, remove them with a slotted spoon, and place them on paper towels to drain. Dust them with powdered sugar. Serve warm.

STORAGE INFORMATION: These can be made several hours ahead. Just place them on a towel-lined baking tray...cover them with plastic wrap and refrigerate. Do not freeze. Allow to come to room temperature before deep frying.

PREPARATION TIME: 1 hour

YIELD: 6 servings

ZABAGLIONE
Egg and Marsala Wine Custard

A light and frothy custard you whip up right before their eyes! Just double, triple or quadruple the ingredients to serve the number of guests you have!

1 Egg Yolk
1 tablespoon Sugar
2 tablespoons Marsala Wine
(If unavailable, Straight Sherry
is an acceptable substitute)

Put the sugar and egg yolks in the top of a double boiler and whisk them with a wire whip until they are light and frothy. Place the double boiler (with about ½ inch of water in the bottom section) on the stove over medium heat... whisking continuously. As the mixture begins to warm, gradually add the Marsala, a tablespoon at a time. When the zabaglione is done, it will thickly coat and spoon and lightly mound. Take it from the stove and continue to whisk it for 2 or 3 minutes longer. Serve it warm from the stove, or chilled for up to 3 hours ahead. Mound the zabaglione in tall stem glasses and, if you like, garnish with a few sliced fresh strawberries.

SPECIAL TIP: If you don't have a double boiler, 2 large saucepans, one slightly smaller than the other, will do nicely! Just put an inch or so of water in the bottom pan, and nest the smaller one inside!

STORAGE INFORMATION: Can be refrigerated up to 3 hours ahead, if you prefer to serve it cold.

PREPARATION TIME: 20 minutes

YIELD: 1 serving

GRANITA DI LIMONE O LIMETTA
Lemon or Lime Ice

For purposes of this book, we have listed this recipe in the section on deserts, although at the lodge, we always served these two taste sensations as "palate cleansers" just before the "Piccola Pausas" (or intermissions) between segments of feasting.

For the simple syrup:

2 cups Sugar
2 cups Water
2 Egg Whites
1¾ cups 'Realemon' or 'Realime' Juice
4 drops of either yellow or green food coloring

First make the simple syrup by bringing the sugar and the water to a rolling boil in a large sausepan over high heat. Set the syrup off the stove and let it cool. Refrigerate it over night in a covered plastic container. Beat the egg whites until soft peaks form. Then add the syrup (2¾ cups), the juice and the food coloring. Process for 20 minutes in an icecream maker and then store in a covered plastic container in the freezer.

SPECIAL TIPS: If an icecream machine is not available, you CAN make the granita anyway! Just put the mixture into a covered plastic container and place it in the freezer...going back and stirring it thoroughly every 30 minutes or so, until it is quite firm. The texture won't be quite as smooth, but still quite presentable!

STORAGE INFORMATION: Stores well in the freezer for up to 3 weeks.

PREPARATION TIME: 1 hour

YIELD: 1 quart

BONET AL CIOCCOLATO
Chocolate "Bonnet"

A densely moist and rich chocolate temptation. I found several recipes for this desert...none of which turned out well with any regularity! After weeks of frustration, I finally worked out the right combination! The result is easy and spectacular! While a little more envolved than most of the deserts I've included here, the steps are not difficult, and the result is well worth the time!

4 tablespoons Butter
5 tablespoons unsweetened Cocoa
4 Eggs, seperated
6 tablespoons Sugar
1½ cups finely crushed Amaretto Cookie Crumbs
1 cup Milk
¼ cup Heavy Whipping Cream

For the Caramel:

¾ cup Sugar
3 tablespoons Water
3 drops Lemon Juice
¼ cup additional Water
Freshly Whipped Cream
Marischino Cherries

In a medium skillet, melt the butter. Stir in the cocoa and blend well. Meanwhile, with an electric mixer, beat the egg yolks with the 6 tablespoons of sugar, until it is the consistancy of fluffy cake frosting. Pour the warm chocolate mixture into the egg and sugar mixture and mix well. Add the cookie crumbs, the milk and cream...alternating between the three, until all the ingredients are well blended. Set aside. Whip the egg whites until fairly stiff. Gently fold them into the chocolate mixture until they are completely incorporated. Set aside. Spray a 1½ to 2 quart mold (a souffle pan works well) with vegetable oil pan coating. Place the mold in a large pan with about 1" of water. Preheat the oven to 375 degrees. Now make the caramel. Put the sugar, water and lemon juice in a sauce pan with a heavy bottom. Place it on the stove over medium heat. Stir well to combine, and bring the mixture to a boil. Once large bubbles begin to form in the mixture...stop stirring. Just allow it to boil until it begins to turn a pale golden color. At this point, you will want to tilt the pan gently now and then, in order to help it brown evenly. Don't let it get too dark, or it will harden when it cools. Once it is a nice, even gold color, remove it from the heat. Add the ¼ cup of water all at once...but step back quickly, as it will spatter and boil! Once it settles down, stir the mixture until it is well blended. Pour the caramel into the mold...tilting to coat the bottom. Then pour in the chocolate batter. Place the mold (in the water bath) in the oven and bake until set...about 2 hours...or until a toothpick inserted into the center comes out clean. Remove from the oven, and place on a wire rack to cool for 10 minutes. Then unmold the "bonet" by inverting a plate on the top and (using oven mitts) turning the mold over. The "bonet" will drop onto the plate, and you can then remove the mold. Let cool. Cut into small wedges (this is very rich), and serve either cool or at room temperature...topped with whipped cream and a cherry.

STORAGE INFORMATION: This desert will keep well for up to a week covered with plastic wrap and stored in the refrigerator. Just slice, add the toppings and serve.

PREPARATION TIME: 3 hours

YIELD: 12 servings

TORTA DI RICOTTA AL CIOCCOLATO
Chocolate and Ricotta Cheesecake

A very rich, moist, "New York-style" cheesecake...this one's a real show stopper!

1 cup Amaretto Cookie Crumbs
(crumbled Chocolate Wafers may be used, instead)
¼ cup Butter, melted
2 15-ounce tubs Ricotta Cheese, drained
½ cup Sugar
4 Whole Eggs + 4 Egg Yolks
4 ounces Semi-Sweet Baking Chocolate, grated
1 teaspoon Pure Almond Extract

In a small bowl, combine the cookie crumbs and melted butter. Press them into the bottom of a 9" springform pan, and bake the crust in a pre-heated 350 degree oven for 8 to 10 minutes. Combine the remaining ingredients in a large mixing bowl, and blend at medium speed with an electric mixer until smooth and creamy. Gently pour the cheese mixture into the prebaked shell and return it to the oven for about 1½ hours, or until a toothpick inserted in the center of the cake comes out clean. Remove the pan to a wire rack to cool completely before cutting.

SERVING SUGGESTION: While delicious just as it is, you can also top the cheesecake with a little whipped cream and grated chocolate!

SPECIAL TIP: Before unmolding the cheesecake, run a sharp knife around the edge to loosen. Then, remove the outer ring. Run the tip of the knife between the cake and the bottom of the pan to loosen. Place the cake on a plate lined with a pretty lace doily.

STORAGE INFORMATION: Keeps well (covered) in the refrigerator for up to 1 week. DO NOT FREEZE.

PREPARATION TIME: 2 hours

YIELD: 16 servings

CREMA AL LIMONE
Lemon Cream

A lovely "lemon curd" type filling for tarts and other pastries, this simple recipe makes a delicious spread on toast or English muffins. Since it keeps for several weeks in the refrigerator, a jar of this tangy confection makes a great "hostess gift".

3 Whole Eggs, lightly beaten
2 Egg Yolks
1 cup Sugar
1 stick (¼ pound) Butter
Grated peel of 2 large Lemons
6 tablespoons fresh Lemon Juice

Mix the whole eggs, egg yolks and sugar together in the top of a double boiler, set aside. Grate lemon peel and set aside with lemon juice. Cut butter into small pieces and add to egg/sugar mixture. Stir over medium heat with water in lower portion of double boiler. Add lemon juice/peel. Stir with rubber spatula until mixture thickens to consistancy of a very thick sauce. Remove from heat and place in a bowl to cool. Refrigerate. If you use it as a filling for tart shells or puff pastry cream horns, top them with a dollop of freshly whipped cream and a little grated lemon peel just before serving.

SPECIAL TIP: A good way to tell if the cream is done, is to continue cooking until, when dropped from the tip of a spoon, the cream holds its shape.

STORAGE INFORMATION: Will keep up to 3 weeks in a covered glass or plastic container in the refrigerator.

PREPARATION TIME: 40 minutes.

YIELD: About 1½ cups

PERA CON CIOCCOLATO
Pears with Chocolate Sauce

An elegant recipe you can serve at the conclusion of even the most lavish dinner! Pears poached in white wine and cloves...topped with Mocha Amaretto Sauce.

3 large, fresh D'Anjou Pears, quartered and peeled
1 cup Water
1 cup Dry White Wine
2 cups Sugar
2 teaspoons Whole Cloves
1 tablespoon Lemon Juice

For the Mocha Amaretto Sauce:

8 ounces Semi-Sweet Baking Chocolate
4 tablespoons Hot Water
1 rounded tablespoon Instant Espresso Coffee
4 tablespoons Amaretto Liqueur
½ stick (4 tablespoons) Butter
(cut into small pieces and softened)

In a large saucepan, combine the water, white wine, sugar, cloves and lemon juice. Add the peeled, quartered and cored pears and place them on the stovetop over medium-high heat. Bring to a boil. Reduce the temperature and simmer for 10 to 15 minutes, or until the pears are tender, when pierced with a sharp knife. Remove from the heat and let them cool in the syrup.

To make the sauce: Place the chocolate in the top portion of a double boiler with about ½ inch of water in the bottom portion. Melt the chocolate over low heat. Meanwhile, combine the hot water, instant espresso and Amaretto in a small bowl, mixing well to dissolve the espresso granules. Set aside. When the chocolate is melted, add the softened butter, one piece at a time, stirring well between each addition. Once all the butter has been incorporated, add the coffee/Amaretto mixture and blend well. Place the poached pears in pretty individual glass bowls and top with about a tablespoon of the sauce. Serve warm, or at room temperature.

STORAGE INFORMATION: Both the pears and the sauce can be canned seperately and stored for up to a year. To serve, just warm them in seperate pans (or in the microwave) and serve as usual.

PREPARATION TIME: 1 hour

YIELD: Serves 6

BISCOTTI INTEGRALI
Whole Wheat Cookies Spiked with Rum

Many Italians prefer deserts that are not exceptionally sweet. This cookie has a wholesome, almost nutty flavor that is particularly nice when dipped in coffee or wine! Served after dinner, or for a treat at breakfast, it's sure to please friends and family. (The shaved chocolate on top is optional!)

1 stick plus 2 tablespoons Butter
½ cup plus 2 tablespoons Sugar
1 Egg
2 tablespoons Dark Rum
½ teaspoon Pure Vanilla Extract
2 cups Whole Wheat Flour
1 teaspoon Baking Powder
pinch of Salt
1 ounce Semi-Sweet Baking Chocolate

Cream the butter and sugar in a mixing bowl until light and fluffy. Add the egg, rum and vanilla...beat well with an electric mixer on medium speed. Sift the flour, salt and baking powder, and add gradually to the batter, mixing thoroughly until well blended. The dough should be fairly stiff and easy to roll out. Gather the dough with your hands, and place it on a clean counter dusted with more whole wheat flour. Roll out the dough to a thickness of ¼", and cut with a 2" round cookie cutter. (Gather the scraps and re-roll for more circles.) Bake in a pre-heated 350 degree oven for 8 to 12 minutes, or until firm, and the bottom, a deep golden brown. When done, remove to a wire rack to cool. WHILE STILL HOT, shave the chocolate over the top to melt it into the cookie.

SPECIAL TIP: If the cookies cool off before you have a chance to shave the chocolate over the top...just go ahead and top them with the chocolate in the usual way, and then stick them briefly back into a warm oven!

STORAGE INFORMATION: Stored in an airtight container, these hearty cookies will stay fresh for several weeks...IF THEY LAST THAT LONG!

PREPARATION TIME: 30 to 40 minutes

YIELD: 3 Dozen Cookies

133

TORTA DI GELATO
Ice Cream Torte

A simple desert...that's simply sinful!

2 quarts top quality Ice Cream in your favorite flavor
(Cherry, Strawberry, or any flavor
that includes Chocolate works particularly well for this dessert)
MOCHA AMARETTO SAUCE (see PERA CON CIOCCOLATO)
For the crust:
1 8-ounce package Nabisco Famous Chocolate Wafers
2 tablespoons Butter, melted
2 tablespoons Amaretto Liqueur

Partially defrost the Ice Cream, by placing it in the refrigerator for about 4 hours before assembling the torta. Meanwhile, prepare the center layer...MOCHA AMARETTO FILLING, setting it aside to cool. Next, make the chocolate cookie crust, by crushing the cookies to a fine crumb, adding the melted butter and Amaretto and tossing well with two forks. Press half of the crumbs into the bottom of a loaf pan...reserving the remaining crumbs for the top layer. Next, with a rubber spatula, spread enough of the softened ice cream in the bottom of the pan to come about half way up. Place the pan in the freezer for 30 minutes or more, or until it is frozen solid. Then, take the pan from the freezer, and pour in the cooled MOCHA AMARETTO SAUCE. Level it out, and return the pan to the freezer for about 10 to 15 minutes, or until it is solid. Then fill the pan nearly to the top with softened icecream and sprinkle the remaining cookie crumbs on top, distributing them as best you can, without disturbing the ice cream. Return to the freezer for several hours (or over night) until solid. To unmold this tempting treat, run several inches of hot water in your sink and dunk the pan in the water up to...but not over, the top of the pan. Hold it there for about 5 seconds. Then, gently run a knife around all four sides, and invert the pan onto a piece of plastic wrap and remove the pan. Wrap well and freeze. TO SERVE: Cut into thick slabs and top each with a dollop of freshly whipped cream and some shaved chocolate.

STORAGE INFORMATION: Wrapped in plastic wrap, and sealed in a plastic bag, the torta will keep, frozen, for up to 30 days.

PREPARATION TIME: 3 to 4 hours, including time to freeze each layer.

YIELD: 8 to 10 servings

Le Bevande

Beverages

SWEETWATER WATER SPIRIT

Mineral springs, fumaroles, sulfur extrusions, and even an extinct geyser cone, make of the lodge area a miniature Yellowstone. The creek that courses thru the canyon is named Sweetwater after the clear, cold and sweet springs that are also present.

When we acquired the lodge and began the restoration, the original Sweetwater spring was nowhere apparent. The 1981 flood, considered by the experts "The 100 years' flood", wreaked havoc all up and down the drainage of the north fork of the Shoshone River, including our Sweetwater Canyon.

We carefully went over the records and maps that still existed in an effort to pin-point the exact location of the original spring. No such luck, they were in too general terms. "Sweet" water was going to be wherever we found it by ourselves.

That's when we dis-covered the

Sweetwater Water Spirit that lives in this canyon . . . and still presides over all things wet, to be wet, or were formerly wet!

We dug down about 14 feet in a location we thought most promising and discovered a generous flow of sweet water. We spent several thousands of dollars installing a new and elaborate system, and congratulated ourselves on such good fortune. Within a few weeks we began to notice strange and fascinating things about our water.

We put a pot of water on the stove to boil and within seconds of turning the heat on, tiny bubbles appeared in the bottom, as if it would boil immediately, yet it was still cold.

Turn on any hot water faucet, in any building, and as soon as the cold water started to turn warm, an explosion of air would almost knock the glass out of your hand.

Whiskey and water over ice cubes looked just like whiskey and soda.

What had happened? We now had naturally carbonated sweet water—but not for long. Another week or two passed and the water had a "bite" and began to smell of sulfur. Mineral water had taken over our sweet water spring.

We started a search for another source of sweet water, and in the meantime, hauled drinking water for ourselves and the patrons in our dining room, and took our laundry 35 miles to Cody to do it in the coin laundry. We showered and shaved in mineral water, did the dishes in mineral water, flushed the toilets with mineral water, and watered the lawn and plants with mineral water. In no time at all the tubs, sinks, toilets, china and glassware acquired a green film, the lawn turned white, and the plants began to die.

Climbing over every square foot of ground within reasonable distance of the Lodge, in search of a new spring site, we discovered an ancient catch basin at the top of the cliff in the side canyon behind the lodge. A sweet water flow trickled into the basin, then overflowed down the face of the cliff.

We spent several more thousands of dollars to construct an elaborate piping and cistern system to catch and preserve this new source. Toward the end of August it dried up. We learned it is a seasonal spring . . . normally flowing only April thru August . . . but entirely dependent upon the level of the underground aquifer as to whether it will flow at all.

The Sweetwater Water Spirit was not to be denied. How were we to placate him?

Deciding there was nothing to lose, I cut a green willow branch and began to "witch" a cross-hatch pattern between the lodge and the creek. Near the base of a massive out-cropping of stone that forces the creek to alter course, the willow wand turned downward with such force I could no longer keep it upright. In fact, it literally twisted the bark off in my hands!

We hired a backhoe service to come up and dig for us. After the 4th big scoop came out of the new dig, cold and clear sweet water gushed forth. We fashioned our own well casing out of irrigation pipe and stood it up in the rapidly filling fourteen foot hole, pulled the submersible pump out of the mineral spring, and reinstalled it in our new casing. The trenching, repiping and rewiring, back filling, etc., etc., cost us less than $500.

Is the Sweetwater Water Spirit happy now? Perhaps and perhaps not. You see, while we are still getting wonderfully cold, clear, sweet water from that very same spring, we had to rebuild it and move it closer to the base of the cliff because it was overrun in the flood of '86. Regularly Mr. S. W. Spirit wipes out a water heater, freezes pipes and breaks sewer lines. But we HAVE come to an understanding of each other's space!

BRANNONINI
An Amaretto "Alexander"

We had MORE FUN inventing this one!

2 ounces Amaretto Liqueur
2 ounces Creme de Cacao
1 cup good, rich Vanilla Ice Cream
½ cup Crushed Ice

Combine all ingredients in a blender and process until the ice has disappeared. Pour into champagne glasses and serve.

SPECIAL TIP: For a dramatic effect, rim the glass with sugar first. Just dip the rim into beaten egg white, and then into sugar. Flat saucers work well as containers for both the egg white and the sugar.

STORAGE INFORMATION: Make and serve immediately.

PREPARATION TIME: 10 minutes.

YIELD: 2 cocktails

CAMPARI

Campari, an appertif, was invented in Milan in the 1800's, by a family of the same name. The recipe is a closely guarded secret, but it's slightly bitter taste is thought to come from a combination of herbs and fruit. There are many ways in which you can serve Campari...here are but a few.

CAMPARI AND ORANGE JUICE:

⅓ Campari
⅔ Orange Juice
Ice Cubes

Combine in a tall glass...stir and serve.

NEGRONI:

⅓ Campari
⅓ Sweet Vermouth
⅓ Gin
Ice Cubes

Combine in a 'rocks' glass...stir and serve.

CAMPARI AND SODA:

½ Campari
½ Sparkling Mineral Water (or Club Soda)
Ice Cubes

Combine in a tall glass, garnish with a slice of orange, serve.

HOT BUTTERED RUM

This is a variation of a recipe that was given to me by a friend and fellow lodge owner. Unlike the tradional Hot Buttered Rum that you mix with sugar, rum and butter in a mug with hot water, this is one for a "batter" you can keep on hand in the freezer, that is made extra rich by using ice cream! It's hard to beat one of these on a blustery winter evening in front of a flickering fireplace.

For the Batter:

1 pound Butter, softened
1 pound Powdered Sugar
1 pound Brown Sugar
1 quart Vanilla Ice Cream, softened
1 teaspoon Cinnamon
1 teaspoon Nutmeg

For each mug of Hot Buttered Rum:

1 tablespoon Batter
1 ounce Rum
Boiling Water
Whipped Cream and Nutmeg for topping

You CAN mix the batter by hand...although you may need a friend to help you stir! But if you have one, a heavy-duty mixer (like a Kitchen-Aid), makes short work of this job. Combine all the batter ingredients and mix well. Store the batter in a covered plastic container in the freezer until you are ready to mix your Hot Buttered Rum. Then, place the tablespoon of batter and the rum in a mug, and add boiling water and stir. So that you don't splash the mixture all over the outside of the mug, it's best to fill it only half full...stir well to melt the batter...and then fill to the top with more boiling water, and stir lightly. Top with freshly whipped cream and then add a sprinkle of nutmeg. Serve hot.

STORAGE INFORMATION: The batter will keep for up to 4 months in the freezer.

PREPARATION TIME: Batter: 15 minutes...Hot Butter Rum...10 minutes

APPLE PIE-SANNO

While not very "Italian"...our guests seemed to enjoy it very much on cold, wintery days, when the snow covered up all the fences here at the lodge.

¾ cup Apple Cider
Cinnamon Stick
1 ounce good Canadian Whiskey
(we used Canadian Club)

In a small sauce pan, heat the cider and the cinnamon stick over low heat. Meanwhile, warm a heavy mug with hot tap water. When the cider is very hot, pour the whiskey into the mug and top it with the cider. Garnish with the cinnamon stick. Serve hot.

STORAGE INFORMATION: Make and serve immediately.

PREPARATION TIME: 10 minutes

YIELD: 1 cocktail

GRANATINE DI FRUTTA
Italian Fruit Sodas

YIELD: 1 soda

A very popular non-alcoholic drink, you can vary the flavor with whatever fruit syrup you like. There are a variety of imported fruit syrups on the market (available in gourmet food shops), or you may make your own from things like Chokecherries, Raspberries, Cherries or Blueberries.

2 tablespooons Fruit Syrup
Sparkling Mineral Water (or Club Soda)
Ice
Fresh Fruit for garnish

Fill an 8 ounce glass with ice and add the syrup. Top off the glass with mineral water (or club soda) and garnish with a fresh piece of the fruit used in the syrup (if you have it), or a wedge of lemon or lime...or a sprig of fresh mint. Serve with straws.

STORAGE INFORMATION: Make and serve immediately.

PREPARATION TIME: 5 minutes

WILD CHOKECHERRY DAIQUIRI

The chokecherries grown wild here in Sweetwater Canyon. Early on, we began picking them and transforming them into Wild Chokecherry Daiquiris...much to the delight of our guests! Here's our recipe...now famous around the country.

For the Chokecherry Syrup:
4 cups fresh Chokecherry Juice
4 cups Sugar

For the Daiquiris:
½ cup Chokecherry Syrup
¾ cup Sweet and Sour Bar Concentrate
1 cup Rum (we use Bacardi Amber Label)
About 3 cups Ice Cubes or Crushed Ice

Combine the chokecherry juice and the sugar in a large sauce pan and bring it to a rolling boil over high heat. (At this point, you may want to can the syrup, using traditional canning procedures. In that way, it will keep for a year or more on your pantry shelf.) Chill the syrup in the refrigerator prior to mixing the daiquiris, or it will not make the "slush" type drink this is supposed to be. Then, combine all the ingredients for the daiquiri in a blender. Blend on high speed for about 30 seconds, or until the ice is all incorporated into the cocktail. Pour into suitable glasses, and garnish with either a spiral of fresh lime, or a sprig of fresh mint. Serve.

SPECIAL TIPS: Half the fun of Wild Chokecherry Daiquiris is picking the chokecherries! At this altitude, they ripen about mid-July, and we take a nice sunny Sunday afternoon (or two...we go thru 150 pounds of chokecherries each year!) and make an outing of it! Obtaining the juice is made easy with the use of a steam juice extractor!

STORAGE INFORMATION: Store the blended daiquiris in a covered plastic container in the freezer for up to a week.

PREPARATION TIME: Syrup...10 minutes, Daiquiris...10 minutes

YIELD: 8 servings

INDEX

For additional copies of
FEASTING IN THE FOREST

Write: Dave and Nancy Brannon
Box 7, Cody, WY 82414

Please send me _____ copy(s) of
FEASTING IN THE FOREST
at $10.95 plus $2.00 shipping and handling per copy.
(Wyoming residents also add $.33 state sales tax.)

NAME _____

ADDRESS _____

CITY _____ STATE _____ ZIP CODE _____

Make check payable to FEASTING IN THE FOREST.
Enclosed is my check (or money order)
for $_____.

- -

For additional copies of
FEASTING IN THE FOREST

Write: Dave and Nancy Brannon
Box 7, Cody, WY 82414

Please send me _____ copy(s) of
FEASTING IN THE FOREST
at $10.95 plus $2.00 shipping and handling per copy.
(Wyoming residents also add $.33 state sales tax.)

NAME _____

ADDRESS _____

CITY _____ STATE _____ ZIP CODE _____

Make check payable to FEASTING IN THE FOREST.
Enclosed is my check (or money order)
for $_____.